The
Economist

PUBLICATIONS

Pocket Guide to Advertising

The
Economist

PUBLICATIONS

Pocket Guide to Advertising

Sally King

Basil Blackwell

and

The Economist Publications

Jointly published 1989 by
Basil Blackwell Ltd
108 Cowley Road, Oxford OX4 1JF, UK
and
The Economist Publications Ltd
40 Duke Street, London W1A 1DW

Basil Blackwell Inc.
432 Park Avenue South, Suite 1503
New York. NY 10016, USA

British Library Cataloguing in Publication Data

King, Sally.
  Pocket guide to advertising.
  1. Advertising
  1. Title
  659.1

  ISBN 0–631–15948–7

Library of Congress Cataloging-in-Publication Data

King, Sally.
  The Economist Publications pocket guide to advertising/Sally King.
    p. cm.
    1. Advertising—Dictionaries. 2. Advertising—Great Britain–
  –Dictionaries. I. Economist Publications (Firm) II. Title.
  III. Title: Pocket guide to advertising.
  HF5803.K56 1989
  659.1′03′21—dc19   88–28118 CIP
  ISBN 0–631–15948–7

Typeset in 10 on 12 Bembo
by Opus, Oxford
Printed in Great Britain by
Billing and Sons Ltd, Worcester

For Stephen

Contents

Preface

Advertising is a co-operative activity. Everyone contributes his or her specialist skill or knowledge. Nobody knows it all or does it all on their own. It's just the same for anyone trying to write about advertising. The subject covers such a wide spectrum – from the academic to the practical and highly technical – that you have no alternative to leaning on kindly and long-suffering friends and colleagues who know more than you ever could about their specialist fields. I have shamelessly relied on them, and would like to say thank you to Phil Gullen, Terry Hamaton, Stephen King, Judie Lannon, Patricia Mann, Janet Mayhew, Nigel Newson-Smith, Jacqui Richardson, Toby Syfret and Philip Thomas for taking the trouble to read through relevant entries and suggest improvements. I am also extremely grateful to all the agency people and their clients who gave me permission to use their advertisements to illustrate this book – fuller acknowledgements are in the captions. Thanks also to Rex Audley for adding his wit.

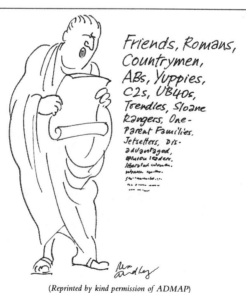

Friends, Romans,
Countrymen,
ABs, Yuppies,
C2s, UB40s,
Trendies, Sloane
Rangers, One-
Parent Families.
Jetsetters, Dis-
advantaged,
opinion leaders,

(Reprinted by kind permission of ADMAP)

Introduction

Advertising is a system of communication whose end-products are advertisements. It is not a sudden manifestation of twentieth-century materialism. Records of its existence have been found in the ancient world – Babylon, Herculaneum – and the Athenian Aesclyptoe is said to have paid the official crier to proclaim this commercial:

For eyes that are shining, for cheeks like the dawn
For beauty that lasts after girlhood has gone,
For prices in reason the woman who knows
Will buy her cosmetics of Aesclyptoe.*

Since the 1880s advertising has had an acknowledged and important role in marketing products and services to consumers, particularly in the development of BRANDS. In 1986 it was estimated to account for 2.4 per cent of GNP in the United States and 1.5 per cent of UK GNP. The past thirty years have seen a lot of changes in the theory, practice and business of advertising, some of which are the response to the necessity in times of recession to improve effectiveness and evaluation.

One such change is the amazing development of the Saatchi brothers' agency during the 1970s and 1980s. In the 1950s, when Madison Avenue dominated the ad world, it would have been unthinkable for a British-owned group of agencies to be the biggest not only in the UK but also in the world. But this is where the Saatchi & Saatchi Group is today. Others are following suit – notably Sorrell's WPP, which swallowed the entire J. Walter Thompson Company world-wide – despite the fact that JWT's turnover, in the last full year before the takeover, was more than 15 times that of WPP. This trend has been accompanied, in both the USA and UK, by a change in the way agencies are regarded by the financial world – once 'professional partnerships', they are now regarded as 'businesses' and performance is judged by City and Wall Street financial standards more than, as in the old days, the quality of their advertising.

Other recent developments are significant. For example, at the beginning of the 1960s the CONVERSION MODELS, Colley's DAGMAR and Rosser Reeves's USP (tested by RECALL TESTS and READING AND NOTING), were generally accepted by agencies and advertisers as the way advertising 'worked' – if it did. In retrospect only three creative men – Bill Bernbach, David Ogilvy and James Webb Young – challenged them at all in their work and their writings.

The first and most basic challenge has been in the new emphasis on consumer responses to advertising, arising from what psychologists have long taken for granted: that communication is a two-way process. The conversion models all assume that input (the content of the ad, wording the proposition correctly) is paramount. The importance of the shift to thinking in terms of consumer response instead cannot be over-emphasized (see ROLE FOR ADVERTISING, REINFORCEMENT, STIMULUS AND RESPONSE THEORY).

A second challenge has been the development of the planning function within advertising agencies (see ACCOUNT PLANNER) which, coupled with the use of computer technology for forecasting (see MARKET MODELLING) provide essential tools for the new models, based on consumer response, of the way advertising works.

A third challenge is the realization that recall is not an adequate test of advertising effectiveness, with the corollary that most advertising is taken in at a very low level of consciousness (see developments in QUALITATIVE RESEARCH, ATTITUDES/ATTITUDE RESEARCH, GROUP DISCUSSIONS, EXTENDED GROUP, PROJECTIVE TECHNIQUES).

More challenges are taking shape. One is the big increase in all forms of communication related to but not strictly defineable as 'advertising': BELOW THE LINE, MERCHANDISING, DIRECT RESPONSE, PR, SPONSORSHIP, etc. This is changing the nature of the ad business and the central position of the agencies within it. A second is the 'fragmentation' effect of the 'new media' – CABLE TV, DBS, VIDEOTEXT – and the use of VCRs which has already begun and which must affect all media planning and research. In the UK there is also evidence of changing public and private attitudes to advertising after a long period of indifference, if not hostility. For example:

● The consumer movement now acknowledges that advertising can be a force which benefits consumers by increasing choice, competition and lower prices (see CONSUMER MOVEMENT).

- Self-regulation of the industry has been effective and the public now has a better understanding of what is and isn't allowed (see ASA, BCAP, IBA CODE OF ADVERTISING PRACTICE).
- Recent research reveals that a significant number of consumers are sophisticated and literate 'consumers of advertising' (see CONSUMER).

This guide also shows how advertising works with and alongside other technologies, for example, film making, print technology, photography and artwork, quantitive and qualitative research, media, computers, etc.

For people who work in advertising it is not enough to understand their own speciality. James Webb Young† (writing in the days when the women's movement was in its infancy) defined the qualities needed to become an Advertising Man. Unlike a lot written about advertising, what he says is as true and relevant today as it was when he wrote it: 'I believe a 'liberal' education to be essential to the full development of the Advertising Man, whether you get that education in school or out of it . . . mastery of the language of words and pictures . . . and the ability to handle mathematics . . . I would invite your special attention . . . to Anthropology. It will teach you to view objectively the societies of man, to understand the 'mold of custom' and other social pressures in them. And in doing so it will help make you the kind of objective penetrating observer of your own society that the Advertising Man must try to be . . . '

A

AA. Advertising Association. A federated body representing the combined interests of advertisers, advertising agencies and media which carry advertising, with well over 1,000 members. Founded in 1926 from the British offshoot of a world-wide Association of Advertising Clubs, the AA today has several important roles, ranging from representing the industry at Government and international level to running conferences and seminars, commissioning research and publications and promoting advertising generally.

The AA has played a key part in the development and enforcement of the self-regulatory code of practice (BCAP) which controls the industry. Both BCAP and its supervisory organization, the ASA, were initiated at successive AA conferences in the early 1960s.

It has an excellent library open to the public and its information centre deals with thousands of requests for information about advertising every year. Its publications include the *Annual Marketing Pocket Book,* a compact but comprehensive collection of marketing data and statistics.

ABC. Audit Bureau of Circulation Ltd. An independent world-wide organization controlled by its membership of over 3,500 advertisers, advertising agencies and publishers. It has operated in the UK since 1931; before that some publishers tried to give trustworthy circulation figures, but many used their imaginations freely. Some, lacking ABC certification, still do.

ABC audits circulations of members' publications and issues regular certified circulation figures (which are also those published in BRAD). Members receive ABC Certificates of Net Circulation.

A 'six-months average' for sales of national newspapers is published quarterly and also shows individual circulations for each month of the period covered.

VFD (Verified Free Distribution Ltd) is a subsidiary company which certifies distribution of publications which do not go through traditional newstrade channels. See FREE SHEETS.

Above-the-line. The advertising spend in media which allow an agency commission, e.g. the press, ITV, posters, cinema. The 'line' however is blurring (see BELOW-THE-LINE, COMMISSION, FEE).

Account. All-embracing term for each brand or client handled by the ADVERTISING AGENCY (see also CLIENT).

Not to be confused with the Accounts Department which deals with the accounting in the normal way.

Account Director. This term is not used consistently between agencies, sometimes not even within an agency. An Account Director can be the member of the Board of the ADVERTISING AGENCY ultimately responsible for the ACCOUNT and for client relations, in particular for developing relationships at the top level. He or she also has responsibility for management of the account within the agency.

Sometimes, however, a person who is a senior account executive is called the Account Director, and the Board member is then the Director in charge of the X account. The client often observes wistfully that almost everyone in an agency is some sort of Director.

See ACCOUNT MANAGEMENT.

Account Executive. The person within the ACCOUNT GROUP with day-to-day responsibility for progressing the ACCOUNT within the agency and for day-to-day relations with the client. Status and title vary between agencies. His (or her: there are many successful women ACCOUNT DIRECTORS or executives) team in a big agency might be a mini-empire of juniors, assistants, etc. In a small shop, the Account Executive can be director, planner and media buyer simultaneously and, when the worst comes to the worst, the entire creative team.

There are many routes to becoming an account executive and you can work your way up from almost any department – traditionally in New York you started in mailing, taking mail and memos round the office. Some agencies recruit from universities and business schools and train up their own executives, others take on people at both junior and senior levels who already have the appropriate experience and need no further formal training.

As advertising and marketing become more complex and

competitive, a would-be account executive must be able to think and analyse strategically as well as having the personality to develop the diplomatic skills indispensable for success.

See ACCOUNT MANAGEMENT.

Account group. (1) The people within the agency who make up the team working on an ACCOUNT. In a large agency, they would include a person, or people, from ACCOUNT MANAGEMENT, the CREATIVE TEAM, the MEDIA department, the ACCOUNT PLANNER (if the agency has them) and probably a progress or traffic controller. Depending on the nature of the account other specialists might be added from time to time. (2) In the USA, account group sometimes means the ACCOUNT MANAGEMENT people only.

Account management. The work done within the agency by the ACCOUNT DIRECTOR and the ACCOUNT EXECUTIVE and their team. It is an extremely difficult and demanding job which involves responsibility for:

- understanding and representing the CLIENT – i.e. the client's values and philosophy, his products or services, his marketing plan, who his competitors and customers are, etc. – to the agency.
- within the agency, getting the right advertising produced – i.e. working with, and inspiring, the ACCOUNT GROUP and especially the CREATIVE TEAM, keeping work and production on schedule. It is not always easy to get all the diverse (sometimes temperamental) people working together productively and harmoniously. Account managers are the impresarios, the Diaghilevs: they have to take the blame when things go wrong and hand out praise when they go right.
- making sure the account is a profitable and viable piece of business for the agency which grows and develops as the client's business does.

Account management has tended to be the way to get to the top of an advertising agency. But it is a high risk job – account managers who lose clients or whose clients turn against them often find themselves jobless.

Account planner. The member of the agency's ACCOUNT GROUP who specializes in planning the advertising strategy. Planners are a comparatively recent addition to agency life. The first Account Planning Department (to be so named) was born in J. Walter Thompson's London office in 1968 and the second appeared shortly afterwards in Boase Massimi Pollitt. Today all top 20 UK agencies have Account Planning Departments, many smaller ones have a planner or two and there is a growth industry in freelance planners. Account planning is catching on throughout the world – even in New York!

Planners have changed the nature of the account group. They have been described* in terms of transactional analysis as playing the adult role between the parents (the account managers) and the children (the creative people). Their aim is to bring all that is known and understood about consumers into the discussion and, in doing so, not only bring the consumer to life but also, in one agency's words, 'to set the creative people free'.

The main role for planners is to take the client's marketing plan and his brief to the agency, and to translate it into specific briefs for creative and media people. Job specifications vary between agencies, but usually include:

● Setting strategies and objectives: (1) for the brand (co-operating with CLIENT and agency ACCOUNT MANAGEMENT); (2) for the advertising (co-operating with account management and CREATIVE TEAM within the agency, as planners usually write the CREATIVE BRIEF); (3) for the media (co-operating with the MEDIA PLANNER).
● Evaluating advertising – principally advising how to measure whether it is achieving the objectives set.
● MARKET RESEARCH – identifying where it is needed, designing relevant proposals, briefing research companies, refining strategies in the light of results. In some agencies account planners even do much of the QUALITATIVE RESEARCH themselves.

An effective account planner needs to combine a good analytic mind with the sympathy, empathy and understanding necessary to work closely with creative people.

See ADVERTISING EFFECTIVENESS AWARDS for published examples of account planners' work.

Added values. The values that people perceive in a BRAND beyond its values as a naked product, service or commodity and for which they are prepared to pay a little more. Some of these added values are functional – improvements in the way the brand performs or what it contains, compared with competitors; some are non-functional or psychological – aspects of design, style and associations that affect the BRAND PERSONALITY. Proof of their existence appears in blind versus named product tests (see BLIND PRODUCT TEST). If brand *A* performs better against brand *B* when the two are named than when they are anonymous, then *A* clearly has some values in people's minds that go beyond the physical product – added values.

Values can be added by product design or formula, extra services, advertising, packaging, naming, pricing, where sold, etc. What matters is how all these are perceived by buyers, and modified by their previous experience, beliefs about the brand and who else is thought to buy it.

Identifying, creating and sustaining added values is a major contribution that an ADVERTISING AGENCY can make to the establishment of a brand.

Adstock. Term coined by Simon Broadbent to mean the total stock of advertising, looked at from the point of view of its effect. Usually applied to television. It assumes that the effect of advertising declines at a regular percentage rate per month, although that rate can vary depending on the market and the circumstances. The remaining proportion of the effect is retained to affect the following month – the CARRY-OVER EFFECT. So the total adstock for a brand in any month is a combination of what is achieved that month and what has been retained from the effect of the previous months' advertising, worked out by nominating a retention rate. In MARKET MODELLING this represents the advertising variable. Alternatively, each month's advertising can be taken as an independent variable and thus the retention rate (or carry-over factor) can be calculated directly.

Advertisement. The product of ADVERTISING. The poster, the TV commercial, the press ad, the radio spot, the cinema ad, the bus side, the tube card: they're all advertisements.

The generally-accepted definition is Jeremy Bullmore's 'Any

paid-for communication intended to inform and/or influence one or more people'.★

Paid-for is essential – you pay for the space or time and you control the content, within the limits of BCAP and the law. Paid-for is what separates advertisements from anything else said/written/filmed about you or your products over which you have no ultimate control. For example, an editorial in a newspaper or Sunday supplement about the bedrooms at Stapleford Park, Bob Payton's new hotel, is not an advertisement. It is an excellent piece of PR.

Advertising exists to communicate and whether it communicates what you thought it would or not, if it is to be an advertisement it must be intended to communicate something. It doesn't matter whether an advertisement is intended to communicate with one person (Charming woman seeks entrepreneurial man, photo appreciated) or several (Two utterly groovy Goths seek others into Sisters) or millions (Vote Labour). They are all advertisements.

Advertising agency. Specialists in creating advertising. Originally space brokers, who bought space from media, sold it to 'clients' to fill, and took a percentage as commission. James Walter Thompson was allegedly the first man to take the next step and begin advising his clients how to fill it to their advantage. This was in New York in 1864. Advertising agencies developed from his idea.

These beginnings account for agencies' legal position today as principals – an agency buys the space and bills its clients, being, for example, liable for unpaid bills if one of them defaults or goes bankrupt. Today the commission system is being challenged by Restrictive Trade Practices legislation (see COMMISSION). Media Trade Associations and the individual media operate a recognition system – before an agency is entitled to commission, its financial and professional capability is investigated.

There are over 1000 self-styled advertising agencies in the UK today employing around 15,000 people altogether. Over 90 per cent of advertising placed through agencies comes from the 300 who are also members of the IPA.

Agencies vary as much as individuals: there is no blueprint. They vary in size – some employ over 500 people, many under

50, some under 10; in organization – some provide the full range of services (see FULL SERVICE AGENCY), others only a very basic in-house service, calling in outside people (see CONSULTANTS) for account planning, media planning and creative work as necessary; in the business they attract – some agencies specialize and

James Walter Thompson, founder of JWT and the advertising agency business as we know it, in his favourite off-duty role as Commodore of the New York Yacht Club. With acknowledgements and thanks to the J. Walter Thompson Company Ltd.

handle only, say, direct mail, financial advertising or local business accounts, others hog the big 'national' accounts.

So, for an advertiser, choosing an agency is a matter of research to find the agency whose services and personalities match your needs and personalities. Liking the creative work is only one factor, others are:

• Big agencies tend to get the big accounts from big companies, if only because there have to be enough people in the agency to 'match' all the people at the client's end.

• There has also been the convention that an agency does not take on accounts for competing products. Conglomerates (like Saatchis) can get round this by being organized as several parallel and/or subsidiary agencies which are run separately from each other.

• The most important difference is between their priorities, philosophies and methods of work. 'A very important part of what differentiates them (agencies) is their differing view of how advertising works'.★

Many of today's top ten agencies have been up there for years, but every generation has its own ideas so that new small agencies are constantly being started up. The current London crop is

US agencies' worldwide billings, 1986

		$m
1.	Young & Rubicam	4,191
2.	Saatchi & Saatchi Compton Worldwide	3,320
3.	Ted Bates Worldwide	3,262
4.	BBDO Worldwide	3,259
5.	Ogilvy & Mather Worldwide	3,155
6.	J. Walter Thompson Co.	3,142
7.	McCann-Erikson Worldwide	2,853
8.	DDB Needham Worldwide	2,558
9.	D'Arcy Masius Benton & Bowles	2,259
10.	Foote, Cone & Belding Communications	2,155

Source: Advertising Age (Advertising Age figures cover only US agencies)

UK agency billings 1987: agencies' own figures

		£m
1.	Saatchi & Saatchi	257.00
2.	J. Walter Thompson	222.00
3.	Dorland Advertising	210.14
4.	Young & Rubicam	154.00
5.	Ogilvy & Mather	145.00
6.	D'Arcy Madius Benton & Bowles	130.00
7.	Boase Massimi Pollitt	125.90
8.	Lowe Howard-Spink	120.40
9.	Grey	115.30
10.	McCann-Erickson	112.60

Source: Campaign

UK agency billings, 1987: Media Register figures

		£m
1.	J. Walter Thompson	163.18
2.	Saatchi & Saatchi	163.06
3.	Dorland Advertising	128.49
4.	D'Arcy Masius Benton & Bowles	111.53
5.	Ogilvy & Mather	100.97
6.	McCann-Erickson	92.30
7.	Young & Rubicam	79.71
8.	Lowe Howard-Spink	75.20
9.	Collet Dickenson Pearce	74.16
10.	Boase Massimi Pollitt	71.39

Source: Campaign

Agencies' own figures use definition of billing as: 'total of the sum spent on advertising above and below the line, by all clients, and for which the agency was responsible in the period 1 January to 31 December 1987.' Media Register figures are for press and TV advertising only and do not include radio, direct mail, below-the-line or outdoor advertising. The comparison between the two sets of figures does not therefore measure how much everybody lies about their billing, but the difference between the type of work done; e.g. further figures show that JWT is far ahead on TV billings, but only fourth (to Saatchi's lead) on press.

known as the 'Third Wave'. Saatchis (founded in 1970 and now the biggest world-wide group) has made the agency business financially respectable.

See also ACCOUNT DIRECTOR, ACCOUNT EXECUTIVE, ACCOUNT MANAGEMENT, ACCOUNT PLANNER, CREATIVE DEPARTMENT, MEDIA BUYER, MEDIA PLANNER, PROGRESS DEPARTMENT.

Advertising Effectiveness Awards. Biennial competition started by the IPA in 1980. Papers, submitted by individuals (usually planners) from ADVERTISING AGENCIES, assess and evaluate the measurable effects of one advertising campaign. Prizes are awarded on methods of assessment, measurement criteria, clarity of argument, but not creative content. The four books of winning case histories edited by Simon Broadbent and Charles Channon provide the most convincing analyses of the relationship between sales and advertising available to date.★

Advertising idea. All of us ignore most of the communications that bombard us continually; to remain sane we simply phase them out subconsciously. Advertisements, in particular, get a low level of attention. So advertising people believe that, if their work is to get noticed at all, it must stand out from the crowd. How successful that work is depends on the advertising idea.

Nobody is too precise about what they mean by this. But, just as editors know what makes a good story for their paper, advertising people get a feel for a good advertising idea. Bill Bernbach's maxim, 'Do it different' still holds for most. A favourite credo is his other 'It's not just what you say that stirs

This Black Magic Campaign, which started in 1935 and ran in more or less the same format until the late 1950s, used the simple device of a partly-seen letter and the picture of the girl writing it to add a romantic dimension to the chocolates. The idea expressed perfectly the added values which set the brand apart from its competition. The girl always reflected the ideal of her time (this ad ran in the Audrey Hepburn epoch) so the campaign was long-lived. With acknowledgements and thanks to Rowntree Mackintosh and the J. Walter Thompson Company Ltd.

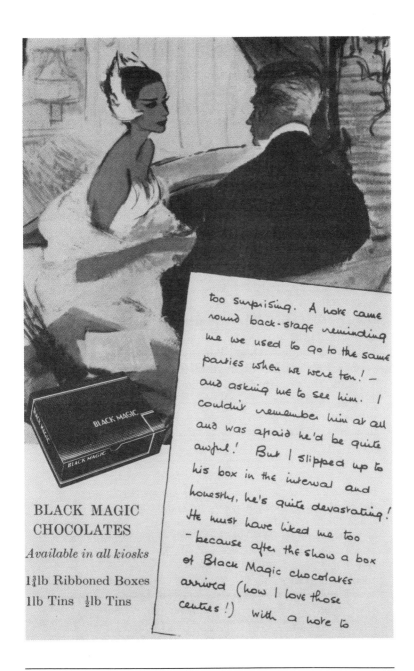

BLACK MAGIC
CHOCOLATES

Available in all kiosks

1¾lb Ribboned Boxes

1lb Tins   ½lb Tins

too surprising. A note came round back-stage reminding me we used to go to the same parties when we were ten! — and asking me to see him. I couldn't remember him at all and was afraid he'd be quite awful.' But I slipped up to his box in the interval and honestly, he's quite devastating! He must have liked me too — because after the show a box of Black Magic chocolates arrived (how I love those centres!) with a note to people. It's the way you say it'. David Ogilvy says 'you will never win fame and fortune unless you invent *big ideas'* and that it helps you to recognize one if you ask yourself:

1   Did it make me gasp when I first saw it?
2   Did I wish I had thought of it myself?
3   Is it unique?
4   Does it fit the strategy to perfection?
5   Could it be used for 30 years?

But he adds you could count on your fingers the campaigns that last as long as 5 years.* James Webb Young described an idea as 'nothing more nor less than a new combination of old elements'. He worked out his technique† for getting one. First, gather the raw material, partly from the information contributed by the planners and any research. Second, carry on the 'mental digestive process' of constantly thinking about the problem. Third, go away and do something else (like Sherlock Holmes taking Watson off to a concert) when, fourth, the idea will come out of nowhere. Fifth, more work shaping and developing the idea to practical usefulness. David Bernstein says 'the idea becomes an advertisement largely as a result of craft'.‡ Young also adds helpfully 'the principle of constantly expanding your experience both personally and vicariously, does matter tremendously in any idea–producing job,' – good advice for any creative person in an agency today (see COPYWRITER).

Bernbach's famous series of ads for VW put the Beetle on the map in the USA and inspired a whole generation of creative people to emulate their style. He followed his own maxim – 'do it different' – by featuring the car itself, which was in complete contrast to the vast gas-guzzling monsters in favour at the time, and by using provoking, almost non-selling, headlines to capture the reader's interest. He exactly caught the mood of the intellectual minority who were beginning to rebel against conspicuous spending with conspicuous thrift. The copy line was always rational but people who bought the Beetle had (and still have) an emotional commitment to it. With acknowledgements and thanks to Volkswagen (UK) Ltd. and DDB Needham.

Think small.

18 New York University students have gotten into a fun-roof VW, a tight fit, the Volkswagen is sensibly sized for a family. Mother, father, and three growing kids suit it nicely.

In economy runs, the VW averages close to 50 miles per gallon. You won't do near that, after all professional drivers have canny trade secrets. (Want to know some? Write VW,

Box #65, Englewood, N. J.) Use regular gas and forget about oil between changes.

The VW is 4 feet shorter than a conventional car (yet has as much leg room up front). While other cars are doomed to roam the crowded streets, you park in tiny places.

VW spare parts are inexpensive. A new front fender (at an authorized VW dealer) is

$21.75.* A cylinder head, $19.95.* The nice thing is, they're seldom needed.

A new Volkswagen sedan is $1,565.* Other than a radio and side view mirror, that includes everything you'll really need.

In 1959 about 120,000 Americans thought small and bought VWs. Think about it.

Often the advertising problem is less about getting ideas than about judging which among many ought to be developed. The point of all the careful planning (see ACCOUNT PLANNER, CREATIVE BRIEF, ROLE FOR ADVERTISING) beforehand is to define objectives against which the creative ideas have to stand or fall.

The Heineken campaign is an outstanding example of how a successful advertising idea can be developed over a long period of time and used equally effectively on posters, TV and radio (see SCRIPT). The old Black Magic letter campaign and the appropriately sparkling Perrier campaign illustrated on pp. 15 and 19 are two other classic examples, as are many of the other advertisements shown in this book.

It must be said, however, that advertising people often differ in their criteria for judging advertising ideas – as is demonstrated by the comments of the nine top creative people Barry Day asked to choose and explain their favourite ads in his collection of great advertisements. ★★

AGB. Audits of Great Britain Ltd. An important UK market research conglomerate. It runs, among many activities, a number of continuous CONSUMER PANELS (Television Consumer Audit, Attwood Consumer Panel, AGB Personal Purchases Index, among others). AGB also currently holds the contract for BARB.

The Perrier campaign is based on a very simple advertising idea brilliantly executed. The visual and verbal puns on which it is based are invariably captivating. The campaign is an object lesson in how to give a product the added values by inference so that it gets the right responses from consumers. The readers/viewers perceive, or have their opinions reinforced, that Perrier is chic, fun, up-market, acceptable. (Whereas when this is spelt out in so many words as, for instance, to say 'It's chic and fun to drink' it is totally unconvincing.) With acknowledgements and thanks to Perrier (UK) Ltd and Leo Burnett Advertising.

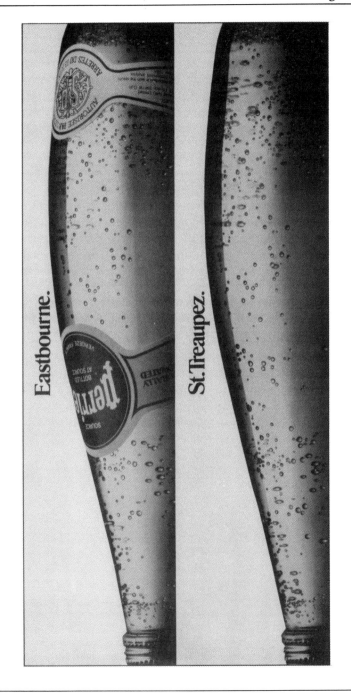

AIDA. Ancient mnemonic for one theory about how communication works. So, for those who still believe that communication is a one-way process, it provides a check list for judging advertisements. AIDA says, in effect, that successful advertisements should, in this order: get Attention, hold Interest, arouse Desire, obtain Action.

See also CONVERSION, CONVERSION MODELS, STIMULUS AND RESPONSE THEORY.

Animatic. Somewhere in between a STORYBOARD and a filmed TV COMMERCIAL. Made by selecting key frames of a highly-finished storyboard, photographing them as stills with a rostrum camera, adding a soundtrack and cutting to length. This can give quite a realistic impression of the final film, but is much cheaper to produce than a proper film.

Animatics are useful to research consumer reactions before embarking on actual film production; to sell an idea to a client; to present a preview of a campaign at a sales conference.

(Reprinted by kind permission of ADMAP)

Animation. Film technique used for cartoon films to make drawn characters or inanimate objects, models or puppets move. Each frame is drawn, or set up, and filmed separately in sequence so when the film is run the movement is lifelike. Computer animation, an example of which is the Channel 4 station identification signal, offers elaborate new possibilities.

Answer print. Also known as check print. The first print of the completed film, as finally agreed. Submitted by the processing laboratory to the production company, so the quality can be checked before the final bulk print order is produced.

Appropriation. The annual amount the client allows (appropriates) for advertising out of his marketing budget. Appropriations can be set in various ways. For instance:

- What's available after all other costs in the budget have been met. The disadvantage of this is that to treat advertising as a residual is to ignore its whole commercial purpose; this can affect the sales on the 'top line' and thus profits on the 'bottom line'.
- Using a fixed advertising/sales (a/s) ratio. The ratio is usually set by tradition, so is not always appropriate for changing circumstances.
- Matching competitors in spend or a/s ratio. Unilever's Dynamic Difference model is a more complex method. Evidence from Nielsen shows that successful brands tend to have a share of advertising above their share of market.
- Task method. Expenditure is calculated to achieve specific objectives. This avoids rule of thumb, but has disadvantages: either the task can be related to advertising expenditure but is still remote from business objectives (e.g. brand awareness), or the task is realistic (e.g. profits) but it's very hard to relate the appropriation to it.
- MARKET MODELLING. If the data provided are good this can show interrelated effects of a large number of factors all together and over a long period of time, making judgements of past advertising effectiveness and likely short-term returns on different levels of expenditure possible.

Whatever method is used, the 'right appropriation' is a matter of judgement, based on the current long-term and short-term marketing objectives for the brand.

Art buyer. Responsible for commissioning artists, photographers, design studios, everyone producing finished ARTWORK. The Art Buyer also keeps records and sees portfolios, putting together short-lists of possibles for the CREATIVE TEAM.

Art director. Person responsible for the visual aspect of the agency's work (see CREATIVE TEAM). An Art Director does not have to draw like an angel, but it helps to be able to wield a pencil with confidence – most have some art, design or graphics training. Some may have specifically studied film and eventually become TV producers. The job varies from agency to agency. Naturally some art directors dominate their accounts, while others do not, but all must be able to work with other members of the team. The Art Director's contribution is usually:

● Co-operating with the creative team to develop any ideas visually and take responsibility for their execution.
● Producing the rough layouts, STORYBOARDS, mock ups, etc., which will initially sell the ideas within the agency, sometimes to the client.

This famous 'Persil washes whiter' campaign was indebted to its Art Director for his idea of contrasting the whiteness of the plain paper or poster with the light screen on the 'other' non-Persil-washed garment. This ad ran in 1955, when the claim was still allowed. Persil advertising, unlike a lot of other detergent and washing powder advertising, has always been perceived as friendly, and as having a genuine understanding of the way wives and mothers see their role in family life. With acknowledgements and thanks to Lever Brothers and the J. Walter Thompson Company Ltd.

● Briefing whoever is being commissioned to do the finished ARTWORK, make the film, etc. This involves keeping up with new films, TV, publishing, the art world generally, since choice of the artist, film director or photographer could make or break a creative idea. Plus keeping up with new technologies which also affect how an idea can be developed.

● Taking responsibility for details of visual presentation. Art directors are involved in choice of locations, models and actors, props. They attend the shoots. They spot talent by looking at portfolios and show reels.

Art Directors get peer-group approval with the annual Designers and Art Directors Association Awards when their ideas are judged on visual brilliance above all.

See also ADVERTISING IDEA, CREATIVE BRIEF, CREATIVE TEAM, LAYOUT, ROUGH, STORYBOARD, TYPOGRAPHY, TV PRODUCER.

Artwork. All illustrations (photographic, drawn or painted, black and white or colour) and special lettering in their final form ready for processing for reproduction.

Polo posters have developed and elaborated their well-established slogan, 'the Mint with the Hole', into a whole series of visual puns like this one for their poster campaigns. These are very much Art Directors' campaigns, though, as here, there is usually a verbal pun to crown the idea. With acknowledgements and thanks to Rowntree Mackintosh and the J. Walter Thompson Company Ltd.

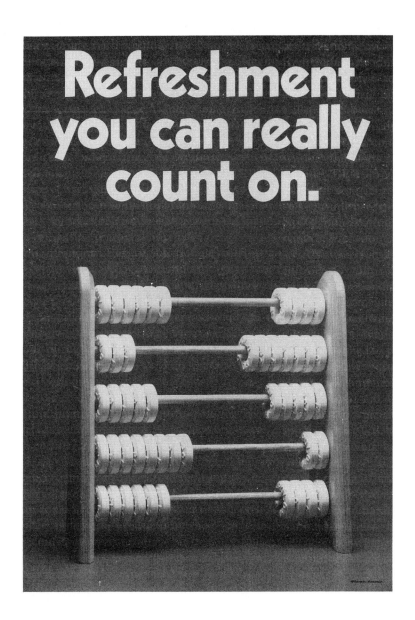

ASA. Advertising Standards Authority. Set up at the 1962 AA Conference to take up the vital supervisory role in the industry's new system of self-regulation for non-broadcast advertising. Unlike the IBA, which performs a similar role for broadcast advertising, the ASA is not a statutory body. It is a limited company, financed through the Advertising Standards Board of Finance Levy on Advertising.

Tremendous efforts are made to ensure the independence of the ASA and that it could never become, or be mistaken for, a pro-advertising lobby. The Chairman and the majority of its 12 council members must, for example, be entirely unconnected with any advertising interest.

The ASA's role is to monitor the work of the CAP Committee in drawing up and revising the British Code of Advertising Practice and British Code of Sales Promotion Practice, and to deal with intra-industry complaints. One independent ASA council member sits on each of the CAP Committee's specialist sub-committees.

ASA enforces BCAP. Up to now, the UK has not found it necessary to follow the example of such countries as Canada or Sweden and set up, and pay for, a statutory framework for print advertising, and our system is considered to have worked well. When the EC Misleading Advertising Directive comes into force in 1988 there will be an ultimate legal back up. But the terms of BCAP and its day-to-day administration will remain the same. Enforcement to date has depended not only on ASA's attention being drawn to transgressions of the Code, but also on an active monitoring programme. Since 1975, at the instigation of the OFT, who concluded that if self-regulation were to be as effective

One of the current series of striking Kit Kat posters which are all based on surrealistic visual puns. Here the bar itself becomes the car seats, the wrapper the car's soft top. The situations are always related to the long-established Kit Kat line: 'have a break'. A memorable example of the Art Director's contribution to the advertising. With acknowledgements and thanks to Rowntree Mackintosh and the J. Walter Thompson Company Ltd.

a deterrent as legislation the Code needed to be more widely known and public awareness increased, the ASA has been energetically publicizing BCAP. Free space is donated by newspapers, magazines and poster companies for the advertising campaign.

Today about 2,000 complaints a year are investigated by ASA. They have to be sent in writing. If an advertisement is found to have been in breach of the Code, it has to be withdrawn and/or amended. Should the advertiser refuse to do this, the media who support the ASA will not accept it for publication. Case reports are published regularly and are available free.

ASA also commissions research, runs an information service and actively promotes standards in the industry generally.

One of a new series of advertisements produced by the ASA to publicize the existence of the BCAP and get the public to respond by informing the ASA of any infringements, or ads they think are straying from the legal, decent, honest and truthful path. With acknowledgements and thanks to the Advertising Standards Authority.

Advertisements are expected to conform to rules and standards laid down by the Advertising Standards Authority. Most do. The few that don't we'd like you to write in about.

And if you'd like a copy of these rules for press, poster and cinema advertisements, please send for our booklet. It's free.

The Advertising Standards Authority.
We're here to put it right.

ASA Ltd., Dept. Y, Brook House, Torrington Place, London WC1E 7HN.

This space is donated in the interests of high standards of advertising.

Attitudes/Attitude research. If one accepts that advertising has to elicit responses rather than hammer in messages (see REINFORCEMENT, ROLE FOR ADVERTISING, STIMULUS AND RESPONSE THEORY), consumers' attitudes are as important to an advertiser as their age, social class and residential neighbourhood – especially so if the advertising is aiming to reinforce existing attitudes – the 'How right I am to do/buy/think/vote this way' response – or modify them – to bring a brand up to date for example.

The concept of attitude has been worked over at length by academic social psychologists since the 1920s, who use it 'to designate inferred dispositions, attributed to an individual, according to which his thoughts, feelings and perhaps action tendencies are organised . . .'.⋆ Simple everyday advertising folk use the word in the sense of 'a set of knowledge, beliefs and feelings about a brand, service or company'.

Researching and measuring attitudes in relation to brands have developed as consumer responses became recognized as the key to effective advertising, and attitudes became linked to a likelihood to purchase. To many marketing people 'attitude research' implies quantitative data, based on respondents' agreement or disagreement with statements, often on a 5-point scale which runs: agree strongly, agree, neither agree nor disagree, disagree, disagree strongly. Statements can cover any opinions or beliefs from healthy eating to capital punishment, childrens' TV programmes to football hooliganism (see LIFESTYLE). This type of research, repeated over a period of time, can measure general trends and changes. Its weakness is that it is rather superficial and at best only reveals conscious, overt, 'public' attitudes.

Today research tries to probe beyond 'public' attitudes, by defining a public/private scale and suggesting different research techniques for different points on it. The conscious, rational, 'public' attitudes, accessible to QUANTITATIVE RESEARCH are one end of it. At the other are the private attitudes – usually sub-conscious, concealed if not repressed – which only skilled, unstructured projective interviewing or observation might reveal (see PROJECTIVE TECHNIQUES). In between are 'personal' attitudes which can, with encouragement from a sympathetic interviewer, be discussed. This involves using qualitative techniques to bring out 'right-hand side of the brain' intuitions, ideas, associations and symbolic values that are expressed through analogy, games, role-playing, etc. These are only suitable for research on a small scale (see QUALITATIVE RESEARCH).

Audio. Indicates the sound track for a film or TV script.

A/V. Audio/visual. Any presentation with both sound and pictures but usually used more specifically for presentations based on slides rather than film. A/V presentations can be very elaborate, using special effects and several screens. They are widely used to brighten up presentations whether at big conferences or for firm's salesmen, and to add depth to art exhibitions and trade shows. Some specialist production companies create only A/V shows.

Awareness. Many advertisers use continuous research to check changes in the proportion of people (or members of a specific target group) who are aware of a brand or its advertising. Figures for spontaneous awareness come from questions like: 'What brands of toilet soap have you heard of? Can you think of any others?' or 'What brand of toilet soap have you seen advertised lately? Where did you see it advertised?' For prompted awareness a list of brands, reproductions of packs or advertisements are shown, and people are asked: 'Which of these brands have you heard of?' or 'Which of these advertisements have you seen?'

There is evidence that brand awareness is a good measure of SALIENCE and frequency of purchase. So where the ROLE FOR ADVERTISING is to jog the memory about a frequently purchased brand, it can be a measure of the effectiveness of the advertising.

But the use of awareness of advertising as a measure of its effectiveness has always been controversial. Some advertisers have used it as their main measure, but the published evidence is against them. Most agency people regard it as at best a very subsidiary measure, often of dubious relevance; they think its popularity is due in part to its being easy research to carry out. It is often linked with recall and recall testing (see RECALL TESTS) which are equally questionable as measures of effectiveness, but can be helpful diagnostically. See EVALUATION.

(*Reprinted by kind permission of ADMAP*)

B

BARB. Broadcasters' Audience Research Board. An independent organization set up in 1981 jointly owned by the BBC and ITVA. BARB commissions the Audience Measurement System for TV (research carried out by AGB) which is used by all interested parties, especially in the advertising industry, and the Audience Reaction Service (research carried out by BRD, the BBC research division) used exclusively by broadcasters and the IBA. Each service is controlled by a management committee representing the users: in the case of audience measurement this includes BBC, ITV, Channel 4, IPA and ISBA representatives. All users contribute to the costs of the service used.

The Audience Measurement System uses a continuous panel of 3,000 homes altogether, between 100 and 350 in each ITV region. Each home has a meter attached to its TV set(s) and VCR(s) which electronically records when the set is switched on and off, to which channel it is tuned and whether the VCR is recording or playing back. In addition all members of the family have their own buttons which they press each time they come into the room when the set is on. There are spare buttons for guests. It counts as 'viewing' when a person is 'present in a room with a set tuned to the channel in question at the turn of the clock minute (providing the behaviour lasts for at least 15 seconds)'. The AGB computer retrieves the information by telephone link between 2.00 and 4.30 a.m. each morning.

Details of programme and commercial transmissions are supplied to AGB by the broadcasters and these are combined with the viewing information to provide audience data.

The weekly TV Audience Report (the Green Book) is published eight days after the end of the week, giving a daily area-by-area chronological record of audiences and ratings to all programmes, commercial slots, commercials and quarter-hour periods, and includes charts of minute ratings for each channel.

The weekly Schedule of Commercials Report (the Blue Book) is published one day later, providing data by brand with product groups, by ITV area, on rate card cost, and with homes', housewives', adult men's and children's ratings for each spot.

An Audience Composition Report is issued three times a year giving detailed demographic information on viewers covering a four-week period.

A weekly press release shows hours of viewing, share of

audience and reach across the network for each channel, as well as listing the top ten programmes for each channel.

In addition, subscribers can be supplied with extra reports and analyses and have access to computer tapes at set fees.

BARB provides the basic tool for scheduling and buying/ selling TV advertising.

BCAP. British Code of Advertising Practice – also referred to as The Code. It is the basis for the advertising industry's self-regulation of all non-broadcast advertising, and it exists alongside, and is supplementary to, all relevant Statutes and Common Law. The first edition was drawn up in 1961, the seventh edition in 1985. The Code is administered and regularly revised by the CAP Committee which is composed of representatives of 19 advertising organizations. There are also specialist sub-committees (see BCSPP). Copies of the Code are available free from ASA.

The Code is based on four general rules, modelled on the International Code of Advertising Practice now accepted by Governments and advertising business in many parts of the world and expressed as follows:

The essence of good advertising

All advertisements should be legal, decent, honest and truthful.
All advertisements should be prepared with a sense of responsibility both to the consumer and to society.
All advertisements should conform to the principles of fair competition as generally accepted in business.

The essence of the Code

The Code is applied in the spirit as well as in the letter.

Part B develops these four points. Part C specifies rules to cover particular categories of advertisement such as Health Claims and Medicinal Products, Hair and Scalp Products, Vitamins and Minerals, Slimming, Cosmetics, Mail Order, Financial Services and Products, Employment and Business Opportunities, Limited Editions, any advertising aimed at Children and requirements from the Media. Two detailed appendices specify the Cigarette Code and rules covering Alcoholic Drinks.

The public is encouraged to complain about any infringements they notice. The ASA deals with complaints from individuals, the CAP Committee looks into complaints from businesses.

See also DECENT, HONEST, LEGAL, TRUTHFUL.

BCSPP. British Code of Sales Promotion Practice. Self-regulatory guidelines, in addition to BCAP, for all sales promotions and advertising for them, covering: 'premium offers of all kinds; reduced price and free offers; the distribution of vouchers, coupons and samples; personality promotions; charity-linked promotions; and prize promotions of all types'.

The code was initiated by the Institute of Sales Promotion, who co-operate with and serve on the CAP sub-committee on Sales Promotion. The first edition was drawn up in 1974, it has now been updated to a fourth edition and, like BCAP, is administered and enforced by the ASA and CAP. The code takes the basic BCAP rules – to be adhered to in the spirit as well as the letter – and applies them to sales promotions in some detail. A video explaining BCSPP is also available. Details can be obtained from the ASA.

Below-the-line. All expenditure promoting the product in ways other than ABOVE THE LINE media. It includes the cost of, for example, COMPETITIONS, COUPONS, DOOR DROPS, FREE OFFERS, JUNK MAIL, POINT OF SALE, PREMIUM OFFERS, PROMOTIONS, SAMPLING, SELF–LIQUIDATING OFFERS. Sometimes 'scheme advertising', promoting the promotion, is also included in an otherwise below-the-line budget. Special promotions designed to galvanize the sales force or provide special inducements to distributors also come into this category.

Billing. Originally the total amount 'billed' by an ADVERTISING AGENCY to a CLIENT, including media and production costs, from which the agency deducted its COMMISSION before passing the money on to the media and the production companies.

Agencies quote their size in terms of their billings, rather than their incomes and revenue. The advertising TRADE PRESS uses billings to work out positions in their agency league tables – their figures, calculated on some arcane formula, provoke intense argument.

Billings are increasingly becoming irrelevant. When agency income was 15 per cent of its clients' total advertising expenditure, billings were a sensible way to measure size and prosperity. Today the commission rate is negotiable and many agencies work on the basis of annually negotiated FEES. When billings are quoted today, the figure is often a notional one, based on what it might have been had the agency been working on a 15 per cent commission. Also work which is not covered by the commission (such as new product development) is given an 'equivalent billing' – the agency credits itself with the billing that would have generated the same amount on the 15 per cent basis.

Bleed. Pages, usually in GLOSSIES or Sunday colour supplements, where the print ad extends to the edge of the page on all sides. Publications charge more for bleed pages. The bleed size quoted is the paper size before trimming.

Blind product test. Products, unlabelled, unidentifiable, un-branded, are tested by consumers who rate them and particular qualities about them in order of preference. This kind of test is used:

- To test the acceptability of a product (usually new or improved) with either the general public or a TARGET GROUP.
- To compare one brand or product against another on performance.
- To compare the performance of a brand when it is not identified and when it is – the difference between the two indicates what the brand's reputation is contributing, or detracting, from its physical characteristics as well as how a brand's added values are perceived.

See also ADDED VALUES, BRAND.

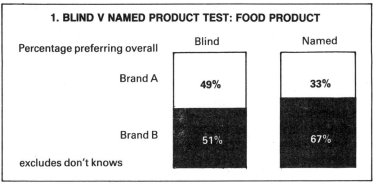

Source: King, 1970

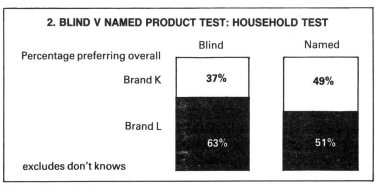

Source: King, 1970

How blind v. named product tests reveal ADDED VALUES. In the household product test brand L did significantly better than brand K when the products were tested anonymously, on their physical and functional performance. But, when named, brand K does almost as well – which indicates the strength of its non-functional added values. In the food product test brand B's added values make even more difference.

Block. Illustrations or photographs to be printed in LETTERPRESS are printed from blocks.

Line blocks only reproduce solid tones. Carved originally from wood, the process which Bewick brought to a fine art, they were later etched into copper by hand. All nineteenth–century magazine illustrations were reproduced this way. They are now made mechanically in zinc and called zincos.

Half-tone blocks reproduce graduated tones, such as photographs. The picture is broken down into varying-sized dots: the lighter the tone the smaller the dots, the darker the tone the larger the dots. The eye accepts the illusion of graduated tones. Black and white illustrations need only one half-tone block. Full colour illustrations need one for each colour – usually four in all.
See also COLOUR SEPARATION, SCREEN.

BRAD. British Rate and Data. Calls itself, accurately, 'the national guide to media selection.' It is published monthly and the June 1988 issue contained 8,313 listings, which included:

- the Press – subdivided into national daily newspapers, Sunday newspapers, regional daily newspapers, weekly newspapers and local free distribution publications;
- consumer publications – over 2,000, divided into subject categories;
- business publications – over 3,500, also categorized;
- TV – including cable, satellite, etc.;
- cinema;
- radio;
- poster;
- every other conceivable medium from London buses to theatre programmes.

Information about each medium includes rate cards, addresses, copy dates, mechanical data and, where applicable, ABC audited circulation figures. All are updated monthly.

Brainstorming. Group sessions with the specific aim of generating new ideas – as many as possible. Participants are heterogeneous (e.g. not members of any particular TARGET GROUP), and the atmosphere is informal to encourage creativity and lateral thinking. The only ground rules are that there should be no negatives – criticism is ruled out; no idea is rejected out of hand because it seems impractical or wildly improbable. Sessions tend to be longer than normal GROUP DISCUSSIONS and may take 3–4 hours.
This technique has been found most useful for generating ideas for new product development.

Brand. Originally the trade mark or symbol that manufacturers put on their products to distinguish them from those of their competitors. As marketing and advertising have developed, the term brand has come to mean the totality of what people buy from a manufacturer or service company. A brand is a unique combination of basic commodity and ADDED VALUES. Lager is a commodity; Carlsberg and Skol are brands, differing both in their functional characteristics (taste, strength, etc.) and in their non-functional values.

Each brand is unique, like an individual (see BRAND PERSONAL-ITY). It is a blend of functional and non-functional values (see EMOTIONAL APPEAL, RATIONAL APPEAL and SENSUAL APPEAL). Its totality is greater than the sum of its parts. Brands can be companies (e.g. Ford, Barclays, Lyons) or single lines (e.g. Alpen, Andrex) or families of lines (Mr Kipling cakes, Fairy soaps and detergents) or retailers of brands (St Michael, Sainsbury). Today manufacturers' brands need to be strong to survive and be profitable alongside PRIVATE LABEL products.

Advertising makes a major contribution to the success of brands. It can not only pick out a brand's key features, but can also communicate its totality to consumers so that the brand is made relevant to their needs and desires.

(Reprinted by kind permission of ADMAP)

Brand image. The total impression people have of a BRAND, built up over the years by the product itself and its associations, both functional and non-functional. The use of the phrase is widespread but as a term it is too imprecise, and used to mean too many different things, to be helpful in analysing or researching a brand's performance. For example, 'image' is sometimes contrasted with 'reality'; but what people feel about a brand is just as real to them as what they sense, taste or see, or the way it functions. Or, when 'image advertising' is contrasted with 'hard-sell advertising', 'image' is used to mean both the total impression people have of a brand plus the physical things created to contribute to this total impression.

In the 1950s, when CONVERSION MODELS and USP reigned, David Ogilvy first put his alternative view: 'every advertisement should be thought of as a contribution to the brand image. It follows that your advertising should consistently project the same image, year after year.' He added, memorably: 'It pays to give most products an image of quality – a First Class Ticket . . . If your advertising looks cheap or shoddy, it will rub off on your products. Who wants to be seen using shoddy products?'.★ This was borne out by the success of the campaigns he then created, for, e.g., Hathaway Shirts, Schweppes, Rolls-Royce, 'Come to Britain'.

He recognized other factors that build a brand image: these campaigns did not run in the up-market *New Yorker* by chance. Choice of media, packaging, retail outlet, etc., as well as advertisements, are all controllable factors on which to build an image. Less controllable are the ideas and interpretations consumers themselves bring to a brand and the effect on them of the other people who buy/use it. Finally, the brand itself: a brand image must reflect the real qualities of the brand (a fact often ignored by politicians polishing up their brand images) because of the contribution consumers themselves make. In spite of Ogilvy, a brand can be very successful on an appropriate third class ticket, e.g. the *Sun* (see PROFILE).

See also ADDED VALUES, BRAND PERSONALITY.

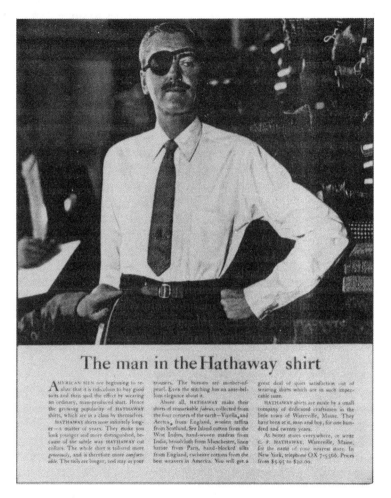

The man in the Hathaway shirt

AMERICAN MEN are beginning to realize that it is ridiculous to buy good suits and then spoil the effect by wearing an ordinary, mass-produced shirt. Hence the growing popularity of HATHAWAY shirts, which are in a class by themselves.

HATHAWAY shirts *wear* infinitely longer—a matter of years. They make you look younger and more distinguished, because of the subtle way HATHAWAY cut collars. The whole shirt is tailored more generously, and is therefore more *comfortable*. The tails are longer, and stay in your trousers. The buttons are mother-of-pearl. Even the stitching has an antebellum elegance about it.

Above all, HATHAWAY make their shirts of remarkable *fabrics*, collected from the four corners of the earth—Viyella and Aertex from England, woolen taffeta from Scotland, Sea Island cotton from the West Indies, hand-woven madras from India, broadcloth from Manchester, linen batiste from Paris, hand-blocked silks from England, exclusive cottons from the best weavers in America. You will get a great deal of quiet satisfaction out of wearing shirts which are in such impeccable taste.

HATHAWAY shirts are made by a small company of dedicated craftsmen in the little town of Waterville, Maine. They have been at it, man and boy, for one hundred and twenty years.

At better stores everywhere, or write C. F. HATHAWAY, Waterville, Maine, for the name of your nearest store. In New York, telephone OX 7-5566. Prices from $5.95 to $20.00.

This is the ad which epitomizes 'brand image' advertising – David Ogilvy's use of the Russian aristocrat Baron George Wrangel who personified social elegance for Hathaway shirts and gave them a unique prestige value. Advertisement by Ogilvy & Mather.

Brand loyalty. A complex and often misleading concept which implies that individuals have exclusive loyalties to single BRANDS in each product field. The more realistic view of shopping patterns – at least for everyday household brands – is that while consumers do have their favourite brands, they also have their own short-list of acceptable brands which they turn to as substitutes. So, in the sense of 'loyalty to Queen and country', total brand loyalty is almost non-existent. See REPERTOIRE.

But there is another category of possessions for which the brand is all-important to the purchaser. Teenagers only feel happy about one particular, essential brand of jeans. Each daily newspaper relies on its cohorts of loyal readers, who feel uneasy and uncomfortable with a substitute. The brand of cigarette offered (see CIGARETTE), the brand of beer ordered are also examples of brands perceived as an expression of the owner's personality and style. This is the level at which brand loyalty is apparent (see PSYCHOGRAPHICS).

Brand manager. The bright young man/woman in the CLIENT company who is responsible for the day-to-day management of the BRAND, and its champion. This is the person the ACCOUNT EXECUTIVE at the Agency normally deals with.

The role of brand manager was introduced into the UK by Procter and Gamble and the originals were grizzled and experienced hands with considerable powers. Now, especially in companies with a big portfolio of brands, the brand manager is comparatively junior and the major decisions on capital investment, marketing budgets, process improvements, formulae, packaging, naming, positioning and so on, are made by his seniors. Brand managers' biggest area of freedom is often over

Another Ogilvy campaign which ran in the 1950s to give Schweppes their first-class ticket to the USA. The very British Commander Whitehead made Schweppes the up-market mixers in American eyes. As the copy consists of rational sales points about the product, the image is a real, not a spurious, one. Advertisement by Ogilvy & Mather.

The ship you see is the *Corinthia*, Cunard Steam-Ship Company Limited

Unloading Schweppes elixir on Pier 92

ABOVE YOU SEE Commander Edward Whitehead, President of Schweppes U.S.A., welcoming still another cargo of Schweppes elixir to America.

The Commander imports this precious essence from England, to make sure that every drop of Schweppes Tonic bottled in America has the *original* flavor. The *curiously refreshing* flavor that has made Schweppes famous all over the world as the authentic Gin-and-Tonic mixer.

Says Commander Whitehead: "It took the House of Schweppes more than a century to bring Schweppes Tonic to its bittersweet perfection. And to develop Schweppervescence—

patrician little bubbles that always *last your whole drink through*."

But it will take you only seconds to mix Gin or Vodka with Schweppes and enjoy the delicious results.

P.S. Add this new drink to your Schweppertory: a jigger of Dry Vermouth over ice and Schweppes Tonic. Tastes almost like champagne!

the creative content of the advertising, and even here their power is all too often to reject but not, finally, to accept.

Even so, the job of brand manager is still an excellent staging post for careers in marketing and advertising, and indeed business management.

Brand name. In a well–designed BRAND all its elements – its name, personality, packaging, advertising, merchandising – should work together. As the brand name represents this totality, naming a brand is important.

Some people believe that the name should express the values of the brand directly, but usually it works the other way round – just as a friend's name takes on his/her personality, a brand name takes on the values of the brand. Bird's Eye now means a special brand of frozen food. Andrex means a premium quality toilet roll. In the USA Edsel came to mean a car you didn't want.

Eventually, when a name is established, it doesn't seem to matter what it is. After long association, maybe accompanied by expensive advertising, but maybe not, a brand name is likely to be perceived as unique. Naming problems arise when new brands are being launched, which have no previous associations. There are four possible strategies:

1 Choose a functional name to explain immediately what the brand is for – e.g. Swatch, Make-A-Meal, Dual, Flushmatic. The disadvantage is that when too many brands in the same product field pursue this strategy, the consumer can get confused – e.g. between Kit-e-Kat and Kattomeat; Sunfresh and Suncrush.

Volvo advertising has many of the qualities of the Ogilvy classics. The product is definitely given its first-class ticket – here with the unmatchable instruments. But at the same time the qualities of the product are brilliantly spelt out, so the consumer is aware of the importance of each technical breakthrough or safety feature and learns to value it. The Volvo 'image' is believable because it reflects reality. With acknowledgements and thanks to Volvo Concessionaires Ltd. and Abbott Mead Vickers • SMS Ltd.

2 Choose a name that has no connection with the brand's function, but could inspire advertising campaigns – e.g. fictional personal names such as Mr Kipling, expressive names such as Smarties, 7–Up, Dr Pepper, Smirnoff, After Eight. A disadvantage here is that the name needs to be established with strong advertising which can work out expensive.

3 Use the reflected glory of the manufacturing company – already famous and trusted in that product field – as an umbrella. This is the Heinz and Kellogg solution, but is only possible if you are this well known.

4 Use the reflected glory of an established brand name as an umbrella for new related products – e.g. Clinique for a whole range of cosmetics for men as well as women. This is only possible for range extensions of an existing successful brand.

Major problems arise for brands sold internationally, and translation is only one of the pitfalls (see GLOBAL MARKETING). In Spanish, Nova means 'no go' and turned out to be an uninspiring name for a car. A lemonade called Pschitt, fine in France, doesn't do in England. Most of the inoffensive names in the main European languages have already been bagged and registered by somebody.

Names and trademarks can be, and are, registered. This gives legal protection against plagiarism, but it is expensive as it is carried out by lawyers specializing in intellectual properties and/or patents.

Brand personality. A more precise, and therefore more useful term than BRAND IMAGE. Brand personality (referred to at Grey Advertising as Brand Character) uses the analogy of people and how they appeal to us. The personality belongs to the BRAND itself, just as it does to people, but it is also a way of expressing our total impressions of the brand.

Brand personality is a very accurate analogy. It makes the point that each brand, made up from physical, functional and associative elements, is a totality greater than its constituent parts; that each brand is unique. Using PROJECTIVE TECHNIQUES similar to those used by psychologists, researchers found that the question 'If this brand came to life, what sort of person would it be?' gave very interesting results. People find it surprisingly easy to 'personalize' products: e.g. 'Tide? . . . A very gruff old man, very fierce. Ex-Army type.'; 'Camay? . . . underneath a bit catty',* thus indicating how real a brand personality can be, and that brands are liked and judged in the same way as people like and judge their friends and acquaintances.

The relevance of this to advertising is:

● Advertising is the one element in the marketing mix that can express the brand personality as a whole. Consistency is important: just as people find it disturbing when a friend acts completely out of character, so they lose faith in a brand with inconsistent advertising, promotions and packaging.

● A brand with a consistent, well-liked personality will be more profitable. The now famous case-history of Andrex (perceived as 'reliable, dainty, clean-living, domesticated, family centred and a nice person to have around the house') shows how, against all odds, a brand can be sold at a premium price in what is otherwise a commodity market.

● When consumers are more affluent, more choice is available and products are more rapidly copied, so brand personality takes on greater significance and plays a more important part in BRAND POSITIONING.

See also ADDED VALUES.

Brand positioning. Placing a BRAND in a specific position compared with its direct competitors in the market-place.

In most markets there are a small number of very fundamental dimensions on which each brand is judged by consumers. Marketing companies decide, from the earliest days of designing the brand, where they want it positioned on these dimensions, especially if they have more than one brand in the market.

The first step is to draw up a MARKET MAP, and position the brands on it according to consumers' current perceptions. This can be the basis for decisions about what new product idea might be successful, or in which direction to try to shift an existing brand, by minor changes in formulation or by a new advertising campaign.

Today many brands, inevitably, are positioned very close to each other. The Ford Fiesta, Fiat Uno and Renault 5 are all positioned as small, fairly cheap hatchbacks; Camay, Palmolive and Lux are mild toilet soaps for every day use. In such cases, establishing a unique BRAND PERSONALITY through advertising is one of the major ways of differentiating one brand from another.

Brand strategy. The complete set of means of achieving a brand's marketing objectives, of which the advertising is one part. Other parts include product development, pricing, distribution, other promotional activities.

See also MARKETING MIX.

Brief. The advertising brief is given by the client to the ADVERTISING AGENCY. It is the client's view of what the advertising is to achieve and how it is to fit into the marketing plan. Ideally, it is a brief and literate summary of what may have been a long process of discussion and analysis. It is important (1) that the advertising objectives are clearly distinguished from the marketing objectives, so the contribution to be made by the advertising is clear; (2) that assumptions about how advertising works are shared by the client and the agency.

The CREATIVE BRIEF is prepared within the agency and agreed with the client at a later stage.

Broadsheet. Newspaper category, based roughly on A1 paper size (approximately 600 mm x 800 mm) folded once. *The Times, Telegraph, Guardian, Independent* and the quality Sunday papers are still broadsheet. Since the mid-sixties most of the popular press have followed the *Daily Mirror* and become TABLOID.

Brown goods. CONSUMER DURABLES destined for the living room, which was supposed traditionally to have all electrical goods in brown (see also WHITE GOODS). Examples are radios, TVs, record players, tape recorders, VCRs, CD systems. All these, of course, have long been available in colours other than brown.

Business-to-business. All forms of promotion by companies selling their goods and services to other companies and/or professional partnerships and enterprises. An estimated £1 billion a year is spent on this through advertising in the TRADE, TECHNICAL AND PROFESSIONAL PRESS, otherwise referred to as the business press, on brochures, on exhibitions, on PR,. on DIRECT MAIL, etc.

This aspect of advertising demands the same quality of strategic planning, the same careful identification of the TARGET GROUP, and the same BRAND coherence as any big consumer campaign. If anything, the RISK factor is higher – when poor decisions mean lower profits. RATIONAL APPEALS are likely to feature most strongly, but it would be a great mistake to think that there is no emotion in business decisions.

B/W. Black and white, as opposed to colour for illustrations, photographs, artwork, etc.

C

Cable TV. The 'wired' alternative to direct over-the-air reception of TV signals. Most cable channels are simply over-the-air land or satellite services which are collected by central receiving antennae and re-distributed across the cable network. Some channels (e.g. local shopping by teletext) are fed into the cable network directly.

In the USA and the UK commercial cable companies operate the network and charge a substantial monthly fee for the channels offered to subscribers. In some European countries cable is treated more as a low-cost public utility, and this accounts for the high level of cable penetration in Benelux and Switzerland.

Potential advantages are: better reception quality and much greater range of channel choice – New York cable offers 48 extra channels in addition to the main networks. The disadvantages are: customer payments and the very high costs and inconvenience of laying cable.

Advertising possibilities being developed in the USA include small-scale test marketing, direct response, home shopping services, 'informercials' – longer, more detailed commercials. Cable has been slow to start up in the UK despite the recent Cable and Broadcasting Bill. By 1987 fewer than 1 per cent of homes were linked up compared with 15 per cent in Europe as a whole.

CAM. The Communication Advertising and Marketing Education Foundation. It is the examining body for vocational qualifications in varying fields of communication, and has, for instance, taken this over from the IPA. The Certificate in Communication Studies covers the whole area of the UK communications business. The Diploma is described by CAM as for 'those who wish to specialise or deepen their specialisation in their chosen career'.

CAM does not run courses; these are provided by colleges of further education, polytechnics and private colleges, of which CAM has a list. It just organizes the examinations and awards. On the whole, it envisages only people already working in the industry, or about to begin, taking the certificate, for which entry requirements are the equivalent to those for university entrance; and only those with some experience in the industry taking the Diploma to develop their specialist/managerial skills.

Nearly all the 'bodies' involved in communication industry are constituent bodies of CAM and support it. Although a vocational qualification may or may not be a help in getting a job in advertising, a lot of individuals currently at the top of their businesses testify to its usefulness to them personally.

Camera-ready. COPY, ARTWORK or a PASTE-UP complete and ready to be transferred photographically for reproduction.

Campaign. (1) Military metaphor covering advertising for a brand or company which is based on the same strategy and creative idea. A campaign can last a few months – say the life of one set of TV commercials – or many years with variations – the 'Persil washes whiter' campaign lasted for over 20 years. (2) Adperson's trade mag.

CAP. Code of Advertising Practice (see BCAP). CAP Committee and its sub-committees draw up and revise the Code and BCSPP. See ASA.

Carry-over effect. The effects of advertising often continue for a long time after the advertisement has appeared. The carry-over effect is the extent to which this happens. It is usually worked out in terms of a retention rate or carry-over factor – the proportion of one period's effect that is carried over to the following period. Such lagged effects have to be taken into account for the advertising variable in MARKET MODELLING.

See ADSTOCK.

Casting. Choosing the 'artistes' – actors, models, animals – for photography and film. Casting makes an important contribution to the establishment of the BRAND PERSONALITY. Over a period of time, characters may have to be subtly recast to reflect the changing norms of daily life. For instance, the original Oxo family which featured Katie and Philip – then a believable sixties family – has now 'grown up' into a more argumentative, older family more typical of the eighties. The Casting Director (employed either by the Agency or by the Production Company) arranges auditions and negotiates fees.

Centre spread. The centre pages in any publication when both pages are printed without a GUTTER, e.g. the centre spreads in *Playboy*.

Charity advertising. Big business for which some very striking and effective advertising has been created.

There are some restrictions: e.g. BCAP, under 'truthful presentation', requires that, if a model is used to create sympathy for a charitable appeal, it must be clear it is a model, not a real person in need. On TV, 'No advertisement may give publicity to the needs or objects of any association or organisation conducted for charitable or benevolent purposes.' But this does not preclude ads confined to giving details of events permitted under the Lotteries and Amusements Act (1976). The question of charities being able to advertise their aims and objects more widely on TV is under review.

Charitable budgets stretch a long way when, as they often are, contributions are given in the form of free space in media, unpaid work, etc. As this is usually a form of DIRECT RESPONSE advertising, its effectiveness is measured by response to each ad.

Children. In 1979 it was estimated that children in the UK had a total direct spending power of £600 million (not including the considerably larger sums their parents spend on them). So they are a considerable market. There is agreement, however, that children's credulity should not be exploited. So advertising directed at children is restricted by both CAP and the IBA CODE. Children (and their parents) are protected by clauses such as:

- no advertising should mislead (i.e. toys and games must be priced and shown in their proper scale);
- no child should be made to feel inferior by not possessing the product advertised;

Two contrasting meal-times for which the casting is all-important for creating exactly the right atmosphere. Above: the Oxo family meal. With acknowledgements and thanks to Brooke Bond Oxo and the J. Walter Thompson Company Ltd. Below: the After Eight dinner party. With acknowledgements and thanks to Rowntree Mackintosh and the J. Walter Thompson Company Ltd.

This is Sarah. She thinks her name is 'Oi'.

'Oi' is all her parents have ever called her.

As if that wasn't tragic enough, there were no toys in the house. Sarah was underweight and not properly clothed.

In fact, when the NSPCC called at the house, Sarah rushed to embrace the inspector. Help had arrived.

The NSPCC's task is to provide help. And with 100 years of practice in cases like this, there's every chance we'll succeed.

But first we have to ensure protection for Sarah.

And that can cost £15.48 for two weeks.

If you can send all or part of that sum it'll be used immediately to help children.

Putting your name on the coupon is the surest way of helping Sarah remember hers.

A heart-rending appeal on behalf of the NSPCC – one of a series in a very powerful campaign which uses realism, what actually happens to a child – to show why it needs the NSPCC to rescue it, and so why the NSPCC needs the reader's help and money. Many charity ads play on the emotions; this one adds a compelling rational appeal as well. With acknowledgements and thanks to Saatchi & Saatchi Advertising.

- advertisers should consider children's safety; no child should be shown doing anything that could lead it into a potentially dangerous situation unless they are 'obviously old enough to be responsible for their own safety'. (There are specific rules about dangerous behaviour, encouragement to talk to strangers in an effort to collect coupons, wrappers, labels, etc.) And so on.

The IBA Code specifies in addition:

- What can and can't be advertised on TV in slots around children's programmes and before 9.00 pm.
- Conditions under which children can be used in commercials or as presenters. (It also promotes 'Good Manners and Behaviour' by insisting children in commercials 'should be reasonably well-mannered and well-behaved'.)
- That health and hygiene should be promoted: e.g. 'advertisements shall not encourage persistent sweet-eating throughout the day nor the eating of sweet sticky foods at bed-time.'

Although most parents curse the latest outrageously expensive electronic toy advertised non-stop for two months before Christmas, research from the USA, Europe and Australia as well as the UK suggests that children themselves, by the time they are 7 or 8, are generally pretty sceptical about advertising claims, especially if they are spending their own pocket money. The Children's Research Unit's work shows that the childrens' family background and their own peer group are important influences on their response to advertisements. In fact, when it is their own money, children will inspect and share their experience before buying more carefully than adults.

Cigarette advertising. Controversial. The anti-smoking lobby wants to ban it altogether. As a result of constraints (both voluntary and compulsory) cigarette advertising today reaches either the heights of ingenuity or the depths of the banal.

The Cigarette Code is agreed between the Government and the tobacco manufacturers, and for all non-broadcast media is administered by CAP. No cigarette advertising at all is permitted on ITV or Local Radio (see also IBA CODE OF ADVERTISING PRACTICE). There are 14 unequivocal rules which include the following:

2.1 Advertisements should not seek to persuade people to start smoking . . .

2.7 Advertisements should not claim directly or indirectly that to smoke or to smoke a particular brand

a) is a sign or proof of manliness, courage or daring

b) enhances feminine charm . . .

2.13 Advertisements should not feature heroes of the young . . .

2.14 Advertisements should not imply that smoking is associated with success in sport. They should not depict people participating in any active sporting pursuit or obviously about to do so or just having done so, or spectators at any organised sporting occasion . . .

Further 'Guidelines for Interpreting the Rules' allow no convenient loopholes. For example:

3.1 Pleasure of smoking (Rules 2.1.3.). In advertisements showing persons smoking, their faces should not express unrealistic enjoyment of the cigarette . . .

In addition, all cigarette display advertisements have to be submitted to ASA's CAP Committee for approval before publication.

Another aspect of control is the obligation to include the Government Health Warning. Since 1982 the amount of space given to the Government Health Warning in any ad has been increased from 9 per cent to 15 per cent, spending on outdoor advertising and cinema films has been decreased, and there has been no further advertising of brands yielding 19 mg or more of tar. Cigarette packets and advertisements have to say whether they are 'low tar' or 'middle to low tar' 'as defined by HM Government'. And the warning words have been strengthened.

Circulation. The ABC definition of a publication's circulation is: 'Net sales which are the bona fide copies bought by individual readers either from the retail point or by direct subscription and represent the audited primary paid readership of a newspaper or magazine.'

See also PASS-ON READERSHIP, PRIMARY READERSHIP, RPC.

Classified ads. Small ads sold by the line and mainly set by the publication in which they appear (as opposed to the advertiser supplying artwork). They are classified under headings, e.g. births, deaths, for sale, wanted, flatshare, overseas travel, personal or St Valentine's Day messages.

For individuals, classifieds are compulsive reading at certain life crises – selling the car or the outgrown Brownie uniform, finding a home help or five nice homes for kittens. The very personal 'Personal' columns are proliferating. Businesses have

---

REVOLUTIONARY PIANO TEACHER MUST SELL convenient S.E.6. 1924 FAMILY HOUSE. 4 bedrms. Drawing rm. takes grand piano. Gd dining rm. 14 ft, kit. Bathrm. Garden a 78 ft. paradise for children and free range guineapig, amidst a plethora of crab (jelly) & cider apples, wine making elderberries & weeds. **GARAGE. REDUCED TO £5,950 FOR QUICK SALE.**

FASHIONABLE ROEHAMPTON VILLAGE. Venerable economist (formerly of the Times) & girl actress/sculptress, SACRIFICE their converted & modernised COTTAGE RES. where sun (south aspect) shines down on them & patio leading to turfed garden with mini fig tree. 2 best bedrms. small third bedrm. for child or dwarf. Drawing rm. & dining rm. Doors between exuberantly torn off to facilitate party flux. Bathrm. & kit. Terrific bargain £6,350 FREEHOLD.

WILL ANYONE TAKE PITY ON A NASTY OLD HOUSE adj. REGENT'S PK.TER. On still nights the friendly howl of the Hyaena floats over the Mappin terraces & one can, maybe, imagine oneself far away from our acquisitive society. 9 rms., 2 bathrms., kit. All in pretty foul order. Will only sell for single occupancy to gentle-people. G.R. £70. Lse abt. 75 yrs. £7250 (I expect we'll see it resold, done up, in a year or so for abt. £14,000).

CHEAP FLAT WITH POSH ADDRESS A retrenching member of the Country Gentleman's Association got as near the soil as he could when he took what is euphemistically termed "the lower ground flr". Still it is fairly light & very cosy & he has assiduously cultivated a crop of chives in a window box. Spacious dble. drawing rm., dble. bedrm., mod. bathrm., lab.–sav. kit. Well dec. in impeccable taste. Lse. 4½ yrs. Only £450 p.a.

Everyone who house-hunted in the 1960s remembers the Roy Brooks ads in the Sunday Times *and the* Observer. *He single-handedly raised estate agent advertising out of the lux.det.res. classifieds and thereby created his own distinct and inimitable brand personality. These are four examples from* Brothel in Pimlico, *a nostalgic selection put together by Tony Halstead and Colin Lowman who keep the business, though not the same advertising, going.*

also found that classifieds pay off. Dealers (who used to masquerade under euphemisms like 'unwanted gift for sale') must now declare themselves. Few, however, have matched the late Roy Brooks for style.

Classifieds provide between 30 and 40 per cent of press advertising revenue; the spend has risen from £461 million in 1978 to £1191 million in 1986.

MEN WANTED for Hazardous Journey. Small wages, bitter cold, long months of complete darkness, constant danger, safe return doubtful. Honour and recognition in case of success – Ernest Shackleton.

The classic classified ad of the sort which appeared when the Times Personal Columns *were on the front page. Ernest Shackleton, the polar explorer, put this in London newspapers in 1900 and is reported to have said: 'It seemed as though all the men in Great Britain were determined to accompany me, the response was so overwhelming.' (Quoted by Julian Watkins,* 100 Great Advertisements, *Dover Books 1959.)*

Client. An advertiser who has been wooed and won by an ADVERTISING AGENCY.

Cluster analysis. A statistical technique for dividing a sample of people into groups, not just on one characteristic (such as age or region) but on a large number of characteristics simultaneously. People in each cluster are not identical on all characteristics, but fit more closely into one cluster than into any of the others. ACORN (A Classification of Residential Neighbourhoods) and Pinpoint are examples of classifications based on cluster analysis.

See also GEODEMOGRAPHICS, LIFESTYLE, LIFE STAGES, PSYCHO-GRAPHICS.

Cognitive dissonance. A psychological concept first related to advertising by Festinger.* He uses as his example the phenomenon that people tend to read ads for the car they have just bought more carefully *after* they have bought it than before. He explained this as their need for reassurance that they have made the right choice.

Psychologists hold that people need their rational, thinking, cognitive self and their emotional, feeling, affective self to be in harmony (consonance) and make considerable efforts to achieve this. Choosing between products, brands or services, can threaten this harmony particularly if the decision is important or expensive, and the alternatives attractive – i.e. you have to keep reminding yourself that you chose the right car.

Cognitive dissonance shows how attitudes and behaviour reinforce each other. Simple CONVERSION MODELS (see AIDA, DAGMAR) of the way advertising works ignore this, which is one of the reasons they are considered over-simplistic.

Colour separation. Preparing illustrations or photographs to be printed in full colour for photo-mechanical reproduction. Colour printing is based on the principle that when the colours in an illustration are separated into the three primary colours (in printing yellow, magenta/red, cyan/blue) and black and then printed in that sequence, almost any colour can be reproduced. Separations are now done photographically using colour filters or by electronic or laser scanning, but getting the balance of each colour correct is still a human skill. Colour separations are checked on progressives – a series of proofs which show how the colours build up. The first is yellow the second yellow plus magenta/red, the third those two plus cyan/blue, the fourth all three plus black.

Commercial. Generic name for any advertising film destined for TV, so-called presumably because originally only the commercial ITV stations could show them!

Commercial TV. TV financed by advertising, as set up by the first Television Act in 1954.
See also IBA, ITV.

Commission. The traditional way clients paid their agencies (see ADVERTISING AGENCY). It was based on the commission (which has varied but is now normally 15 per cent) allowed by media to recognized agencies (only members of the IPA were entitled to take commissions). So if the full price of the space was £100, the agency would be charged £85. The bill (see BILLING) passed to client would have to have 17.65 per cent added in order to bring the amount the agency received up to £100. The same percentage was added on to production costs. So the agency received 15 per cent of the total costs.

FEES are becoming preferred to the commission as a method of payment, for several reasons: a lot of work done by agencies was not covered by the commission; on 15 per cent very small advertisers do not pay their way, and very big advertisers tend to feel too much profit is being made from their business; many agencies were not members of the IPA and so not entitled to the commission.

The final demise of the commission system was hastened by the Restrictive Trade Practices legislation in the 1960s, the simultaneous growth of MEDIA INDEPENDENTS and the growth of small agencies offering only a limited range of services. The norm now is for clients to be charged a fee, the amount of which, ironically, is often based on the old 15 per cent. Some agencies (the more competitive or more desperate for business) offer cut-price services at a much lower rate.

Comparative advertising. Ads which compare one BRAND against another or others. They are seldom believed to be fair by the 'other brand'. There is some evidence from the USA that comparative advertising may be distasteful to consumers and counterproductive in that it makes them suspicious of both brands and even of advertising itself. But 'in order that vigorous competition may not be hindered and public information may be furthered' (BCAP), comparisons are permissible – even to the extent of naming other firms and comparing prices, which some car advertising has been doing from time to time, usually to show what good value a particular model is in its price range. The battle of the lawnmowers over the past few summers in the UK is an example of how far comparisons can legally go. But there are still some conditions:

1   The comparison must be fair and not mislead.
2   The basis of the comparison must be clear.

3   Evidence must be substantiated and the general unsatisfactory nature of the 'other brand' not contrasted with selected advantages of the brand being sold.
4   Price comparisons can be made, but not when savings are manipulated in favour of the brand advertised.

Competitions. Promotions/advertisements which offer contestants prizes, on the basis of their skill and judgement, *not* by chance or 'gratuitous distribution'. As the idea is to create excitement around your BRAND, the prize must be amazing, relevant and advertiso-genic. Cars you wouldn't normally think of affording and trips for the day on Concorde are examples of recent competition prizes.

Creating, running and advertising a competition is fraught with rules and regulations. The BCSPP starts its section on 'Promotions with prizes' with a severe warning:

---

1   Legality
Most commercial promotions with prizes are subject to legal restrictions. Before embarking on any such scheme, promoters are strongly advised to seek expert legal advice. Attention is particularly drawn to the Lotteries and Amusements Act 1976 and relevant case law.

The BCSPP then details conditions of entry, availability of results, advertising, handling, free draws, games of chance.

There has been no recent research evaluating the effectiveness of competitions. There is supposedly a hard core of people who go in for competitions all the time. A 1966 survey found that although they appealed particularly to younger housewives (half the entrants were under 34) they also appealed to almost everybody else, i.e. AB, C1 and C2 people (see SOCIO-ECONOMIC CLASSIFICATION)

Competitions are also being used by DIRECT MAIL to add excitement and, one suspects, to refine MAILING LISTS.

Concept. A concept can be like a PROPOSITION, and express the main benefit(s) of the brand, service or product to the consumer in a straightforward and factual way (see USP). In that case it is likely to be limited to a RATIONAL APPEAL only – e.g. Hovis is a traditional brown bread, more nourishing, fibre-full, etc., because it is made from entire grains of wheat. Or, a concept can incorporate an EMOTIONAL or SENSUAL APPEAL, if it is possible to put this into straightforward, factual language, – e.g. Hovis embodies the traditional virtues of good natural food and a good healthy way of life as embodied by our vision of rural England a hundred years ago because it is made the traditional way, etc.

When agencies or manufacturers talk about the 'key concept', the term may be used in either sense, but implies that this is the basis for the advertising, either current or being planned. So in the case of Hovis a few years ago, the second proposition, rather than the first, would have provided the springboard for their series of nostalgic pastoral TV commercials.

Concept testing. Since a CONCEPT is by definition not an advertisement, concept testing is criticized because consumer reactions to the concept are not necessarily an accurate prediction

I'm the Office Manager, Account Executive, Media Buyer, Creative Director, Senior Planner and Coffee Maker on Tuesdays

of their reactions to an advertisement based on the concept. Nevertheless, concept testing goes on.

Consumers selected from the TARGET GROUP are shown concept boards and answer a series of questions and/or give comments. A concept board may just consist of a written-out concept, or it may include an illustration, a pack shot and even some copy. But obviously it does not embody an ADVERTISING IDEA, because the concept is what is being tested not the advertising. Responses to concept tests therefore tend to be at a rational level at the expense of the emotional and/or sensual level.

See CREATIVE DEVELOPMENT RESEARCH.

Consultant. In the advertising world, any specialist or small group offering limited and clearly defined services. Top-level strategic planners, packaging experts, freelance creative people and many more count as consultants. Consultants are also people called in to give expert or professional advice, e.g. doctors for medical products or vets for products sold for pets or farm animals. They are paid *ad hoc* or, occasionally, kept on retainers.

Consumer durables. Manufactured goods which are 'durable household goods'. The Family Expenditure Survey's main categories are:

- Furniture
- Floor coverings
- Soft furnishing and household textiles
- Radio TV and musical instruments
- Gas and electrical appliances
- Other appliances
- China, glass, cutlery, hardware, etc.

Cars are normally excluded. As all these are supposed to be long-lasting, relatively expensive and therefore infrequent purchases, buying patterns are different from FMCG and so is the role of advertising.

See also WHITE GOODS, BROWN GOODS.

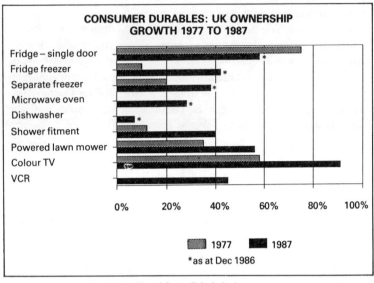

CONSUMER DURABLES: UK OWNERSHIP GROWTH 1977 TO 1987

Source: AGB Home Audit, Audits of Great Britain Ltd

Some examples of the way things that are at first thought of as luxuries become 'normal possessions'. The changes over the past 30 years are even more marked than these which represent a random selection of changes over 10 years. For example, it is extraordinary to remember that in 1960 the majority of homes did not have a fridge, let alone a freezer.

Of course, the biggest change of all is ownership of the most 'durable' possession of all – the home. Home ownership is estimated to have increased from 33 per cent in 1957 to 60 per cent in 1987.

Consumer movement. Consumerism became focused in the UK in the 1960s with the foundation of the independent Consumers' Association (CA, publishers of *Which?*, now the Association of Consumer Research and still in the forefront of many consumer battles). Today consumers' interests attract greater Government attention: the Office of Fair Trading was set up in 1973, the NCC (National Consumer Council) in 1975 and there is a Minister of State for Consumer Affairs.

Consumerism can no longer be dismissed (as it was by one US businessman in 1967) as 'of the same order as the hula hoop – a fad'.

Initially the consumer movement was opposed to advertising, on the grounds that it encouraged people to buy things they didn't need and couldn't afford, put prices up, stifled competition, misled if not deceived people, etc. But views that advertising might stimulate competition, bring prices down, give useful information to the consumer, etc., are now gaining ground, backed up by US experience such as the lowering of opticians' charges once they started advertising. The general public has never revealed such reservations about advertising. A series of surveys commissioned by the AA demonstrates this.

The NCC works for consumers generally. The new Chairman, Sally Oppenheim Barnes, has identified three important issues: the reform of consumer rights under the Sale of Goods Act; public and private monopolies; unjust credit terms.

The Consumers' Association led the successful fight to allow lawyers to advertise, on the grounds this would give consumers the benefits of better information and greater competition. Their legal adviser, David Tench, said: 'There's only one thing worse than misleading advertising, and that's no advertising at all.'

Pressure from the consumer movement as a whole has led the Government to initiate some controls and restrictions, e.g. the Cigarette Code and the Price Marking (Bargain Offers) Order (see OFT). The IBA describes itself (see IBA CODE OF ADVERTISING PRACTICE) as 'one of the country's official instruments of consumer protection' through its control over the content of all broadcast advertising, as well as that of the programmes of course. The current Chairman and Deputy Director of CA have both served on the ASA Council.

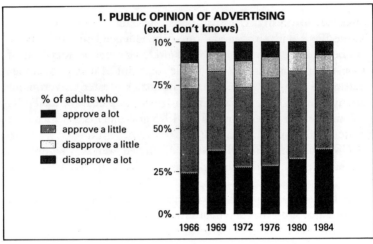

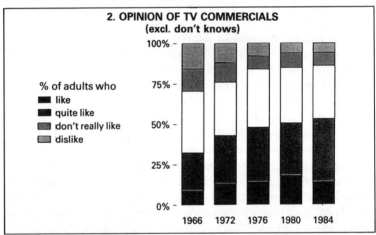

Source: Advertising Association

These diagrams show how advertising now only arouses intense hostility from a decreasing minority – since even the TV commercials are 'liked' or 'quite liked' by just over 50% of people compared with under 15% who 'dislike' or 'don't' really like' them.

All the same advertising is a topic of low importance to most people – far below the Government, Education, Trade Unions or Politicians for instance in the sense that people say they talk about them, hold strong opinions about them and/or feel they need immediate attention and change. In fact most advertising has to fight inertia rather than over-reaction – see ROLE FOR ADVERTISING.

Consumer panel. A representative sample of consumers selected to record their purchases of particular types of products or services over a period of time. Consumer panels are widely used as a regular measure of market share. Whereas RETAIL AUDITS measure aggregates, consumer panels reveal individual behaviour patterns – e.g. REPERTOIRES, number of different brands bought, frequency of buying, prices paid, etc.

There are several continuous syndicated consumer panels (e.g. Taylor Nelson's Family Food Panel, AGB's Television Consumer Audit) which cover large numbers of product fields. Clients buy into them. There are also short-term consumer panels (e.g. the National Food Survey) which require people to record buying and using patterns in some detail for a specific period – say four weeks. A wide variety of *ad hoc* panels are set up for specific jobs (e.g. CONSUMPTION STUDIES or for evaluating new brands and/or price experiments).

Consumers. Everyone is a consumer. We all consume products and services even if someone else buys them for us. From the advertiser's point of view the definition is narrowed down to people who do or might at some time buy their particular BRAND, either for themselves or their families.

Advertising people spend a great deal of time, effort and money investigating consumers – their needs, desires, fantasies, responses, lifestyles, incomes, children, dreams, eating habits, time in front of the TV, etc. And what they buy, and how often, and whether they recall advertisements. All in the interests of producing advertising that works. What has only just begun to be reckoned with is that consumers are consumers of advertising as well as everything else.

Recent research shows that many consumers, far from being passive and helpless recipients of advertising, are both sophisticated and literate about what advertising is for, how it works and how they respond.* For example, younger people, who have grown up taking TV for granted, are particularly perceptive.

GROUP DISCUSSIONS about TV commercials demonstrated this in many ways:

1 Their explanations of how advertising 'works' included: by association of ideas – providing a trigger at the point of sale; by entertaining you – you are more receptive because you enjoy the advertisement; by including guilt – you feel you are not living up to the 'ideal' families/lifestyle in the commercial.

2 Their awareness of ASA rules, what can and can't be said. In spite of this, for some commercials there is a credibility gap, especially concerning testimonials, because obviously 'people are paid to say what they are told'.

3 Their identification of 'styles' of TV commercials irrespective of products being advertised – among them: nostalgia, cartoon, humour, surveys, fantasy, health, moral, sexy. Within commercials their recognition of whose voices were used in voice overs, techniques, etc.

4 Their appreciation of advertising which is involving and entertaining, in a conventional sense, and also defined as 'different', 'intriguing', 'well-made', 'powerful', *not* 'boring', 'dull', 'uninteresting', 'weak'.

The implications for advertisers are that if the consumer is a consumer of advertising as well as the brand advertised, this is another dimension to consider when creating and evaluating advertising.

See also ROLE FOR ADVERTISING, STIMULUS AND RESPONSE THEORY, CONVERSION MODELS.

Consumption studies. Asking the person who uses, or consumes, rather than the person who normally buys, e.g. children about certain foods and snacks rather than their mothers, or secretaries, rather than the firm's finance director, about office equipment. It can be in the form of question-and-answer research, but is more often based on diaries kept by a panel of consumers.

Contact report. Or Call Report. Names for the report issued by the ACCOUNT EXECUTIVE after each meeting with the CLIENT, which minutes decisions/discussions. This is the way most ADVERTISING AGENCIES keep track of work and progress. Not to be confused with a Status report, which is normally a general summary of where the work on an account is at the time, rather than a report of a meeting.

Contacts. In the technical sense, the first sheets of negative-sized prints which a photographer sends to the ADVERTISING AGENCY after a photographic session so a few can be chosen for enlarging and showing to the CLIENT.

In the general sense, anyone you've met who might be useful.

We've done extensive
research into the way
the name is perceived

Controlled circulation. Specialist publications, not sold on the open market but sent directly to members of a Trade Association, club or professional society, have controlled circulations. Many, except the most learned journals, are delighted to take advertising, but few if any have audited circulations.

Conversion.
1   Sales term: converting leads into sales.
2   Direct response term: converting requests for information into sales or leads, or, with recruitment advertising, into good quality leads.
3   Advertising theory: direct conversion of consumers to buy your brand instead of their usual one after seeing the ads. Now considered an over-simplification of how advertising can work.
See CONVERSION MODEL, REPERTOIRE, REINFORCEMENT.

Conversion model. Model of the advertising process which implies that it works by the direct conversion of the consumer from buying brand *A* (always) to buying brand *B* (always). Such models usually imply that the conversion is achieved by rational persuasion. Underlying all views on how to produce good advertising and all methods of 'testing' advertising is some model of how advertising works. Conversion models have been very pervasive, from the quite simple – such as USP or AIDA – to the quite complex – such as DAGMAR.

However, there is much evidence that advertising rarely works by conversion. People have REPERTOIRES of brands, and most advertising seems to work by REINFORCEMENT or modification of existing patterns of behaviour.

This is one of the ads which made the Saatchis famous when they started up their agency (it was actually written by Charles Saatchi). Nobody could ever read it and feel relaxed about a fly buzzing round the kitchen again, it's such a powerful piece of writing. The fact that it is reversed out makes it, if anything, more revolting. With acknowledgements and thanks to Saatchi & Saatchi Advertising.

This is what happens when a fly lands on your food.

Flies can't eat solid food, so to soften it up they vomit on it.

Then they stamp the vomit in until it's a liquid, usually stamping in a few germs for good measure.

Then when it's good and runny they suck it all back again, probably dropping some excrement at the same time.

And then, when they've finished eating, it's your turn.

Cover food. Cover eating and drinking utensils. Cover dustbins.

The Health Education Council

Copy. Originally, all the words to be set in type by the printer. In advertising today it includes all the words to go in an advertisement, on a poster or package or to be spoken in a TV, radio or film commercial. Supposedly original, *not* copied.

Copy date. Time/day by which advertising material is required for a particular issue of a publication. Always specified on the RATE CARD.

Copy platform. Term used in the 1950s to describe the central basis of the content of an advertising campaign. CREATIVE BRIEFS now use a term such as CONCEPT, KEY FACT or single-minded proposition.

Copywriter. Member of the CREATIVE TEAM responsible for the COPY, and who works closely with an ART DIRECTOR to generate and develop ADVERTISING IDEAS.

No specific training ensures success as a copywriter. Literacy and an ability to write the finished copy whether it be for a TV commercial or a detailed brochure is expected. Wit is an optional extra. The ability to analyse a problem and pursue an argument convincingly is essential, as is an eclectic range of interests.

Back in 1913 the anonymous writer of an 'Advertisers' Pocketbook' described the qualifications of an ad-writer as follows: 'first . . . a keen student of human nature so he may know how to appeal successfully to different classes of people.

This is a totally different way of writing copy. Rolex had previously been majoring in their advertising as watches for the world's most powerful men – Presidents, Prime Ministers, and such like – who were at that time all men. This series was created in the 1960s to persuade women to respond to the idea that a Rolex could also be a very feminine accessory. Making it a feline one too, with the stylish drawing (rather than a photograph of the model of the year) made it eye-catchingly 'different'. With acknowledgements and thanks to Rolex Watch Company Limited of Geneva and the J. Walter Thompson Company Ltd.

It wasn't fascinating to know the time –until she had a Rolex

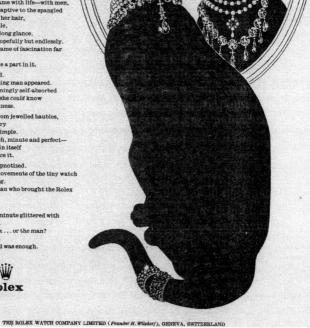

Bewitched
By her own loveliness
And bewitching, too,
She played a game with life—with men,
Making them captive to the spangled
   gleaming of her hair,
Her fateful smile,
Her heady sidelong glance.
They waited, hopefully but endlessly.
She knew the game of fascination far
   too well
To let time take a part in it.

Things changed.
A silent, watching man appeared.
He saw her seemingly self-absorbed
But knew that she *could* know
A subtler happiness.

Seducing her from jewelled baubles,
   silken flattery
Was swift and simple.
One Rolex watch, minute and perfect—
So fascinating in itself
She *had* to notice it.

Now *she* was hypnotized.
To watch the movements of the tiny watch
Became exciting.
To watch the man who brought the Rolex
   to her
Was the same.

Each diamond minute glittered with
   significance.
Was it the Rolex . . . or the man?
She didn't care.
To be fascinated was enough.

Rolex

THE ROLEX WATCH COMPANY LIMITED (*Founder H. Wilsdorf*), GENEVA, SWITZERLAND

73

Second, analytical faculties well developed . . . Third, ability to write interestingly, clearly and convincingly.' Seventy years on, David Ogilvy* describes six hallmarks of a good copywriter 'Obsessive curiosity about products, people and advertising . . . A sense of humour . . . A habit of hard work . . . The ability to write – interesting prose for printed media, natural dialogue for television . . . The ability to think visually . . . The ambition to write better campaigns than anyone has ever written before.'

The major change in requirements, caused by the growing importance of TV, has been the necessity for copywriters to have or develop strong visual understanding.

Most copywriters work as part of a CREATIVE TEAM or Group in an AGENCY; a few work freelance, often as part of an informal team. A copywriter may, or may not, play a part in developing the CREATIVE BRIEF – the basis on which work is done.

Corporate advertising. Advertising by companies/corporations/ conglomerates to affect people's awareness of and attitudes to the organization as a whole rather than the products or services it offers. As such it is nothing new. Blue-chip companies in the USA (Du Pont, General Electric, AT&T) began what was then called 'prestige advertising' in the 1930s.

The development of the corporate communication industry is a relatively new response by companies to the challenges of their economic and social position today, and advertising is just one channel of communications within it. David Bernstein's* wheel

Shell's corporate communications have included many distinguished advertising campaigns – among them the Shell Guides to different parts of the British Isles. Shell has long had the reputation of a 'good source' and with this ad continues the theme of a company that cares about the countryside. It is a dramatic and effective demonstration of the way a pipeline need not ruin the environment it runs through – and the lengths Shell goes to restore its original beauty once the work of laying it is completed. After seeing this ad, would one be so worried at the prospect of a pipeline crossing one's view or favourite landscape? With acknowledgments and thanks to Shell and Ogilvy & Mather Advertising.

of company communications consists of nine audiences (internal, local, influential groups, the trade, Government, the media, financial, customers, general public) which can be reached through any or all of nine channels (the product, correspondence, PR, personal and impersonal presentation, literature, point of sale, permanent media, advertising).

Olins† has developed the idea of Corporate Identity – and the contribution made by the visual design of everything, from the factory to the product to the logo – as 'the glue . . . that will express to everybody with whom they deal what they do, what they are, what they stand for' (see CORPORATE LOGO).

Theodore Levitt‡ has drawn attention to the important 'source effect' on communications: 'the audience's feelings about the credibility of the message source help determine the persuasive effectiveness of the message itself.' More and more companies are recognizing the value of having a reputation as 'a good source'. Among many benefits, they see improved morale and recruitment, better relations with the local community, support from local and central government and planning authorities. Investors large and small invest in their shares, and in take-over battles their shareholders support them.

In addition, the company behind a BRAND is particularly important in the field of expensive infrequently-bought consumer goods (cars, etc.), technically-complex goods bought for business or professional use (computers, machine tools) and in service industries where the service is used intermittently (airlines, insurance).

Corporate advertising has to bow to the same disciplines as any other advertising. Alan Wolfe** identified 10 specific ground rules:

1 Set realistic objectives and specific goals.
2 Be consumer-oriented.
3 Start early, i.e. don't wait for a crisis.
4 Define the target audience.
5 Plan – for research-based evaluation.
6 Be informative, candid and credible.
7 Keep an important, recognizable, flexible format.
8 Merchandise the campaign, particularly to employees.

9   Be consistent. Plan for the long term.
10   Involve top management. The BRAND MANAGER has to be the Company Chairman.

Sometimes companies have not started early enough (see 3 above) and faced by a crisis (threat of nationalization, takeover, expensive new processes demanded by environmentalists) react with advertising to rally public opinion. The lesson to be learned from the masterly campaign run by the clearing banks in the 1970s (The Banks Debate) is, having analysed what response was required, to treat the public as intelligent adults and involve them.††

Corporate logo. See also LOGO. Companies/corporations which make different products under several brand names often like to have a logo to identify the parent company.

The ICI roundel has an important role in the company's strategy to establish a strong corporate identity. The company manufactures and markets a wide range of products throughout the world, and the roundel is designed to be the visible link between all its high-tech products, its medicines, fertilizers and synthetic fabrics. The way it is used is strictly controlled, even to the exact shade of blue it ought to be. This version was re-designed in 1987 – a modification of an original which had previously had a re-vamp in 1969. With acknowledgements and thanks to ICI.

Coupon. Device to nudge the consumer more positively into buying. Coupons are used in particular for:

- DIRECT RESPONSE advertising. The coupon is the key when the aim of an ad is to get the consumer to fill it in, cut it out and send it off for the brand/product. The effectiveness of the ad is judged on the number of coupons returned and sales made. The design and prominence of coupons has come a long way from the early days (1890s) when an invitation to 'send in at once for . . . ' appeared in tiny print at the foot of the ad. Now with built-in facilities for credit card payment, they are placed to be simple to fill in, easy to cut out.
- DIRECT MAIL. Here too, coupons arriving with the promotional literature are designed to make your positive response easier, especially when accompanied by a freepost envelope.
- MERCHANDISING, BELOW-THE-LINE promotions, whether part of a local test marketing exercise or set up in co-operation with a local retailer, incorporate coupons on the pack or deliver them by a DOOR DROP. The usual offer is 'Money Off' – a bribe to try the product. Even so people forget to exchange them or, worse, commit the sin of malredemption (using their coupons as part payment for the week's groceries without buying the product at all).

NIELSEN run a coupon clearing service to help manufacturers and retailers.

Couponing. The act of delivering coupons to households in a selected area.

Coverage. The extent to which advertising reaches its TARGET AUDIENCE. Net coverage or reach is the proportion/percentage of the target audience who have been exposed/had an opportunity to see/hear your advertising at least once within a specified period.

See also EFFECTIVE COVERAGE, FREQUENCY, OTS.

CPH. Cost Per Hundred. A TV reckoning to compare average costs of TVRS for a specific target TV audience.

CPT. Cost Per Thousand. The basic reckoning of the media cost to reach 1,000 viewers, readers or listeners with a given advertisement. It can be applied either to a specific TARGET GROUP or to the total number of viewers, readers or listeners.

Creative brief. The vital piece of paper setting out what the CREATIVE TEAM/group has to produce for a particular CLIENT/ BRAND. It is worked out by the agency and agreed between the client and the agency before work begins.

Many agencies use standard formats which vary in content, complexity and quality. Three thoughtful agencies, *A, B* and *C* include more or less the same information for the same purpose, but in different styles and language:

• Agency *A*'s Creative Strategy Statement includes a description of the target group, the role for the advertising or the hoped-for consumer response, the creative focus (proposition/ key fact) and an evaluation plan.
• Agency *B*'s Creative Work Plan includes a creative strategy covering 'prospect definition', the principal competition, the promise, the reason why.
• Agency *C*'s Creative Brief aims to be a stimulus to creative people; it is not just a description of the task, but also contains details of the target group, role for advertising, key response and brand personality, etc.

Creative department. The 'creatives' in the agency (see ART DIRECTOR, COPYWRITER, CREATIVE TEAM). Its organization varies depending on the size, methods and priorities of the agency. It is headed by a Creative Director (sometimes two – it's a notoriously difficult job) usually an ex-copywriter or art director.

Creating advertising is a group activity and departments are organized into either mixed skill groups of writers and art directors who work with each other in different combinations on different accounts, or creative teams where the same writer and art director are always together.

TYPOGRAPHERS and ART BUYERS are also part of the Creative Department. TV people work closely with the department, but organizational links vary (see TV PRODUCER). Obviously every creative team/group's *raison d'être* is to generate ideas and create advertisements. Another important aspect of their work is to argue coherently for those ideas. One agency managing director is quoted as saying 'The worst thing ever is a creative person who doesn't defend his work with passion.'

Creative development research. Any research used to aid CREATIVE TEAMS/groups in the actual process of developing advertising campaigns. For example:

- Research used as a primary stimulus. Hearing and seeing people talk about their behaviour or feelings about a product type is much more stimulating than reading statistics or computer print-outs.
- Research used to get a quick reaction to a preliminary idea. This can help build on the idea, give confidence that it's on the right lines, or raise quite unexpected snags.
- Research to give an impression of how a finished advertisement might be received.

To some extent all response to ads shown outside their final context are artificial. Creative development research does not aim to measure or predict, but to provide creative people with stimulus and richness of response, so it is nearly always QUALITATIVE RESEARCH (e.g. individual interviews) or GROUP DISCUSSIONS.

Creative team.
1   Today's trend is the creative team – a copywriter and an art director who work together all the time. It is said to be an even more demanding relationship than marriage.
2   The term is also used to include, when making a presentation to the CLIENT, everyone connected with producing the creative work.

CU. Film/TV script shorthand for close up – e.g. a shot of a head filling the screen. BCU (Big Close Up) is even closer in. ECU (Extra Close Up) is closer still – e.g. showing strands of hair.

Cut. Film/TV script shorthand indicating a complete change of shot – the quickest, simplest way to change from one scene to another.

D

DAGMAR. Defining Advertising Goals for Measured Advertising Results – a phrase derived from the title of an influential book by Russell Colley.★

The great value of this idea lay in the emphasis put on the need to set goals for advertising before attempting to evaluate it, rather than rushing in with the latest research technique. It also stressed the need to set goals that are achievable by advertising (rather than by other elements of the marketing mix). Its weakness was its rather rigid underlying model of the advertising process, which assumed people move in a step-by-step way from ignorance of a brand to awareness to comprehension (of a claim) to conviction to action. This is essentially a rational CONVERSION MODEL, and not really suitable for markets in which people regularly buy from a REPERTOIRE of brands.

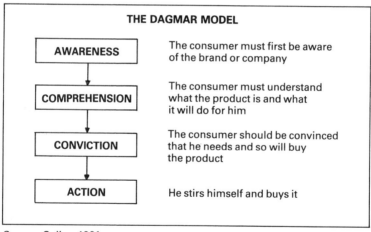

THE DAGMAR MODEL

AWARENESS	The consumer must first be aware of the brand or company
COMPREHENSION	The consumer must understand what the product is and what it will do for him
CONVICTION	The consumer should be convinced that he needs and so will buy the product
ACTION	He stirs himself and buys it

Source: Colley, 1961

DAR. Day After Recall. Method of evaluating the effects of TV COMMERCIALS. People who are identified as having watched ITV at the time the commercial was screened are asked what they can recall about the commercial (usually shown for the first time the day before). DAR is still used in the USA to evaluate commercials, but less and less in the UK as doubts about the validity of RECALL TESTS as a measure of advertising effectiveness have developed.

DBS. Direct Broadcast by Satellite. In its narrow sense, DBS refers to a narrow frequency band-width reserved for *national* 'high power' satellites with sufficient signal strength to permit adequate reception by inexpensive dishes of less than one metre in diameter across the entire country of reception. By international agreement each European country has five DBS frequencies at its disposal. Several European DBS ventures are expected to be launched successfully in the near future. In its broad sense, DBS refers to direct reception by a household antenna, as opposed to land broadcast or cable redistribution. As technical standards have improved, people are beginning to think in terms of reception by flat screens and dishes of less than 30 cm and transmissions from medium power satellites. The first of these is expected to be Luxembourg's private venture Astra, due to be launched towards the end of 1988 or early in 1989, which could carry up to 16 satellite channels simultaneously.

Meanwhile, around 40 channels – some relays of land channels, the majority of private commercial ventures such as Sky and Super Channel – are transmitted by 'lower' power satellites. These depend on cable networks for reception. To date advertising revenues have been limited by a combination of linguistic and cultural differences, restrictive national regulations, low cable penetration and limited advertiser interest in Pan-European opportunities by stations like Sky and Super Channel.

Decent. One of the four key words in BCAP, along with HONEST, LEGAL and TRUTHFUL. Decent is defined in a very general way to cover standards of 'decency and propriety generally acceptable in the UK' which all advertisements must respect. Advertisers are urged in addition to avoid 'unnecessary offence' and to respect the sensitivities of minorities.

A vivid demonstration which shows how a complex argument can be brought to life by an advertising idea. This ad cannot but inspire a heartfelt response from health service administrators, if not from the doctors themselves. With acknowledgements and thanks to ICL and the J. Walter Thompson Company.

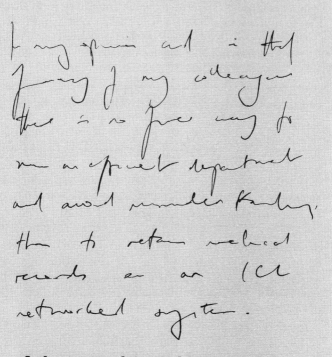

A doctor explains, in his own words, the benefits of computerised medical records.

Running an efficient health service is not just a matter of deciphering doctor's handwriting.
It is important that everyone – nurses and hospital administrators alike – has fast and efficient access to information.

That's why ICL set up the Health Systems Business Unit, whose job it is to help and advise the Health Service, identify any needs they might have and then use their expertise to help solve those problems.

This commitment has resulted in a range of software packages designed specifically for the Health Service. Everything from the Patient Administration System (PAS) to Obstetrics.

And ICL's efficient networking now allows the information this software supplies to be made available wherever it's required – in clear, legible print on a screen.

ICL's Health Systems can readily help you increase departmental efficiency and will also help those departments exchange information more effectively.

One day, perhaps, it may even prove to be the universal cure for doctor's handwriting.

For further information, dial 100 and ask for Freefone ICL.

We should be talking to each other. ICL

The concept is hard to define and necessarily vague as people have such subjective views of what is 'acceptable'. Most complaints to the ASA relate to irrelevant nudity (it's OK to show a nude figure in a shower, but not in a paint stripper ad), or to tasteless, but entirely accurate, trailers for adult videos (which are at least a fair warning of what to expect).

Demographics. Short for demographic variables and originally consisting of those characteristics which were considered most to affect the rates of birth and death in the population. Now used to mean the standard ways of classifying the population (see SOCIO-ECONOMIC CLASSIFICATIONS). The most important demographics are age, sex, marital status, family size, social grade and region. Attempts are constantly made to refine the standard classifications so they are more useful to advertisers (see also LIFE STAGES, LIFESTYLES, GEODEMOGRAPHICS).

Demonstration. Classic approach to creating advertisements which are powerful examples of salesmanship in print or, even better, on TV. This is particularly effective when the ROLE FOR ADVERTISING is to inspire the 'What's in it for me?' response, or the immediate 'Just what I need' response.

It can be corny when done straight – some detergents are demonstrated on TV with the punch line repeated three times. But originality is alive and well: in the treatment of people – the Oxo family commercials which demonstrate the product and the family have been consistently voted 'Best liked commercial' for the past five years (see CASTING); in use of hyperbole – the poster for Araldite with a real car stuck on it (see POSTERS); in original presentation, see ads opposite and on pp. 52 and 147.

Prizewinning ad which demonstrates in the most dramatic way one of a Land Rover's unique selling points and underscores its brand personality in a way nobody else can match. Whichever way you turn the page it makes sense. A triumph of art direction. With acknowledgements and thanks to Land Rover Ltd and TBWA.

Depth interviews. Technique for QUALITATIVE RESEARCH. A small sample is selected, each of whom is interviewed separately. Interviewing follows a loosely structured guide rather than the questionnaire because the aim is to dig into personal attitudes and emotional responses (see ATTITUDES) and encourage ideas, intuitions and associations to emerge. The calibre of the interviewer is the key to usefulness, as he or she not only collects material but also writes reports.

Direct mail. Advertising which is personally addressed and sent through the post to a recipient who may or may not perceive it as JUNK MAIL.

Everybody has noticed how what was a trickle ten years ago has become a flood. Between 1975 and 1983 consumer mailings increased by 154 per cent, business mailings by 29 per cent. The profile of the letter box shows the proportions of different types of direct mail that the average household received in 1987. However, the amount that arrives in households in the UK is still considerably less than in other European countries.

The main advantage of direct mail is that the targeting of prospects can be very exact, provided the mailing list is a good one.

Lists can be built up specially from in-house records; responses to previous advertising or promotions; confidential lists of subscribers; published information (membership lists of professional associations). Or they can be bought from: mailing houses who specialize in direct mail; LIST BROKERS who select from the former; other firms' lists which they may rent out. In 1982 the Post Office introduced its Consumer Location System which enables advertisers, via ACORN, the TGI and the Electoral Register, to locate names and addresses of individuals living in areas likely to contain an above-average proportion of the TARGET GROUP (see GEODEMOGRAPHICS). Post Office surveys show that 62 per cent of people at home and 81 per cent at work 'generally read their direct mail'. An amazing 76 per cent at home and 94 per cent at work 'positively like receiving it *when it is something they are interested in*'.

Creating a convincing direct mail shot is a specialized skill. The effectiveness of every shot can be tested by the response it gets. Agencies, capitalizing on this feedback, have developed as direct mail specialists.

In 1983 the Direct Mail Services Standards Body and Code of Practice was established.

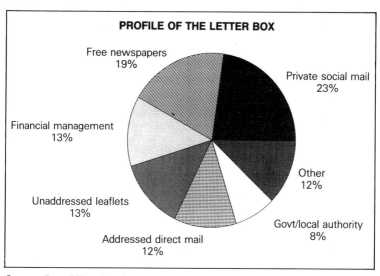

PROFILE OF THE LETTER BOX

- Free newspapers 19%
- Private social mail 23%
- Financial management 13%
- Unaddressed leaflets 13%
- Addressed direct mail 12%
- Govt/local authority 8%
- Other 12%

Source: Post Office Panel, 1987

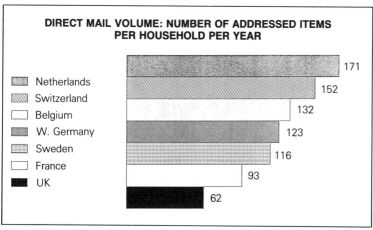

DIRECT MAIL VOLUME: NUMBER OF ADDRESSED ITEMS PER HOUSEHOLD PER YEAR

- Netherlands 171
- Switzerland 152
- Belgium 132
- W. Germany 123
- Sweden 116
- France 93
- UK 62

Source: Post Office, 1985

Direct response. Advertising intended to persuade people to take some form of direct action – either buying goods, sending for a brochure or catalogue, visiting a showroom, making an appointment with a salesman. Appears in all media (now even TV) and includes DIRECT MAIL and much MAIL ORDER.

Its current great success is attributed to:

- The type of products and services advertised, e.g. mini luxuries not widely available in high streets or supermarkets.
- Development of simple payment mechanisms by credit card.
- New media, e.g. Sunday colour supplements.
- Money-back guarantees.

Consumer protection has become increasingly strict. BCAP has a specific appendix dealing with Mail Order, and the Media owners through their associations (e.g. THE NEWSPAPER SOCIETY, NPA, PPA) organize Mail Order Protection Schemes (referred to as MOPS). The worst excesses, such as the advertiser raking in his with–cash orders and then disappearing without trace from his postal address, or even the bona fide supplier so snowed under with orders for what has been advertised that he cannot supply for months if at all, are now illegal. The publishers make sure, for example, that advertisers are financially respectable, that addresses are clearly correct and given and that the likely demand can be satisfied. In certain circumstances they arrange refunds or oblige the advertiser to give them. Even so, the ASA has a special category of complaints for direct response advertising, because there are still so many.

Direct response is the prime example of advertising working by CONVERSION. In theory everything (product, price, media choice, size of space, headline, illustration, copy, caption, coupon, quality of leads) can be tested by analysing response. The earliest analyses of advertising effectiveness were based on direct response. 'The most measurable type of marketing there is', wrote Claude Hopkins in 1923,★ and it still is. Respondents also provide valuable names and addresses for subsequent operations (see DIRECT MAIL).

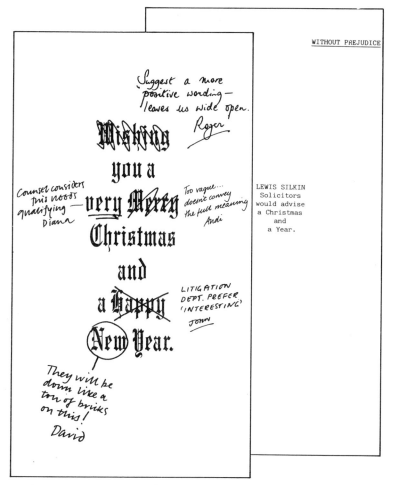

An amusing example of direct mail which has been subtly and appropriately targetted. In sending out this Christmas card, the firm of solicitors give themselves a distinct identity by gently making fun of themselves and their profession: wouldn't we all like to think our lawyers were as human and witty underneath? It is an unforgettable and, to the recipient, a rewarding card to receive, very different from the impersonal run-of-the-mill greetings business and professional people usually send each other. With acknowledgements and thanks to Lewis Silkin Solicitors and The Partners who designed this card for them.

Dissolve. Slow, soft way to change the scene in a film sequence: one shot is gradually faded out while the next is faded in over it.

Distribution. The pipeline through which the manufacturer distributes his products to the consumer. It is the responsibility of the manufacturer's marketing or sales director.

Early advertisers like Levers and Beechams used advertising to build up their national distribution at a time when sales and shops were regionally based. This enabled them to get their goods into shops because of 'popular demand' – a successful example of the 'pull-through' effect. Today special campaigns are directed at distributors, wholesalers, retailers, agents and so on, to persuade them to build up stocks. Expenditure on ABOVE-THE-LINE advertising is considered wasted if a manufacturer has not first created an appropriate and effective distribution pipeline.

Door drop. Couponing, leafleting or sampling households by house-to-house deliveries in carefully chosen areas, if not streets.
See DIRECT MAIL, GEODEMOGRAPHICS.

Double head. Stage in film processing. The visual sequences are cut and assembled in the right order to time on one film; the sound track is on a separate magnetic film. OPTICALS are indicated but not completed. The two films can be projected together for viewing. Adjustments can still be made at this stage.

Double head with opticals. OPTICALS and SUPERS are now incorporated. Adjustments are still just possible. See also MARRIED PRINT.

Down-market. A rather vague pejorative term, deriving from the time when the social class of consumers was the most important aspect of most markets. It can usually be taken to mean that quality has been sacrificed to price, and design/taste aims at the lowest common denominator. Tits and bums are an indication that a newspaper is aiming down-market. Brands often slide down-market by competing on price alone – fruit squashes are examples of brands which have ended up as commodities by following this strategy.
See UP-MARKET.

DPS. Double-page spread – an ad consisting of two facing pages.

Dubbing. Mixing all the different sound tracks together for a film – the voices, the SFX, the music – electronically on to a single magnetic track.

Dummy. Mock-up of, for example, a magazine or brochure which is to be printed. Copy, artwork and visual treatment are generally only indicated, using scrap art and headlines only. Size, quality of paper, binding and cover are as they will be in the finished version, as this is the basis on which the printer quotes a price. The blueprint for the job will have final copy and finished artwork.

Duplication. Media term for the extent to which the audience for one medium overlaps with the audience for another – e.g. the overlap between TV viewers and radio listeners, publication *A* and publication *B*, national and local press.

Dye transfer. Technique for making a specially prepared colour print from a colour transparency which can be re-touched, re-coloured or made up into a montage.

(*Reprinted by kind permission of ADMAP*)

E

Econometrics. Literally, economic measurement, usually the measurement of variables that have a broad economic effect and the interaction of those variables. Or, putting figures to economic theories.

See MARKET MODELLING – the use by marketing and advertising people of econometric methods in consumer markets.

Editing. Key skill in film-making. The editor puts the filmed sequences together into their final order and correct length (see DOUBLE HEAD, DOUBLE HEAD WITH OPTICALS). Editing a TV commercial also involves supervising recording the sound track, DUBBING, post-synchronization, marking up and ordering OPTICALS and, finally, checking the ANSWER PRINTS and (if quality is up to standard) ordering all the prints needed for transmission.

Effective coverage/Reach. The proportion of the TARGET AUDIENCE who have had what is judged to be an effective number/range of exposures within a given period. The number of OTS is a matter of judgement – e.g. a schedule might aim to maximize the number of viewers with more than 2 but less than 6 OTS in 4 weeks. This will depend on the strategy adopted, type of product, creative approach, budget, etc., and the media schedule will be drawn up accordingly.

Emotional appeal. Sometimes expressed as the 'feel' dimension in consumers' response to a BRAND. It is evoked by the style, the mood, the associations and the psychological rewards perceived in the brand, its packaging and the other people using it as well as the advertising. Are the chocs a gift from a man to a woman (Black Magic) or part of elegant dinner party life along with the silver and the cigars (After Eight)? Is the make-up natural, fresh

Another of the famous early Saatchi advertisements. It majors not only on emotional appeal, but emotional shock through telling demonstration. The Health Education Council has a very small budget, but this ad, which first ran in the early 1970s, is still referred to and talked about by advertising people, whatever its impact on its original target group. With acknowledgments and thanks to Saatchi & Saatchi Advertising.

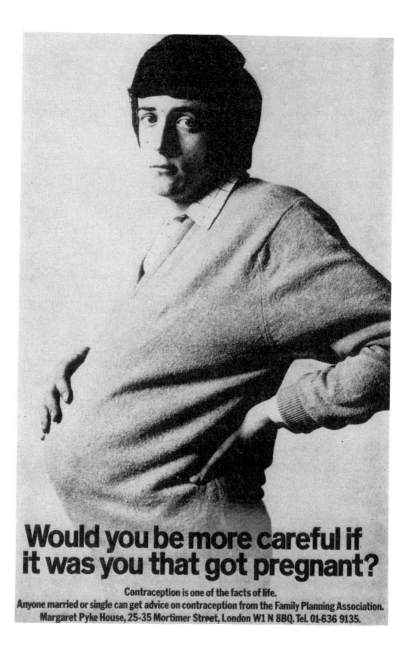

and rather girlish (Body Shop) or sexy, assured and rather Hollywood (Revlon)?

Advertising is frequently used to develop emotional/'feel' responses towards a brand; think, for example, of all those car ads which show the family car in desert or mountainous landscapes (so different from its leafy suburban destination) and which have culminated in the 1988 Peugeot campaign showing the car driving through flames of sugar cane plantation on fire.

Emotional appeal is an element in all BRAND PERSONALITIES but is more dominant in some than in others.

See RATIONAL APPEAL, SENSUAL APPEAL.

Emotional responses are also invoked by much CHARITY ADVERTISING and advertising which is trying to make people change their behaviour/attitudes.

EPOS. Electronic Point Of Sale. The system, just beginning to be taken up in the UK, where bar-codes on the packs are electronically 'scanned' at the check-out. In 1984 1 per cent of groceries were crossing scanners, by 1986 4 per cent were. EPOS is being introduced by Sainsbury, Asda, Tesco and Shoppers' Paradise and the number of installations is expected to double annually. There are many implications:

- For customers – speedier journeys through the check-outs, itemized bills and instant credit checks.
- For retailers – cost-efficient inventory control and re-ordering system, reduced labour costs, better analysis of profitable/less profitable lines, probable growth of private label and so more power over manufacturers.
- For manufacturers – faster, more accurate audits of stocks, sales, effects of promotions, price changes and test marketing. Eventually more pressure on profit margins and the number 2 and number 3 brands. It may become more difficult to launch and/or sustain national BRANDS through advertising. It may also lead to the decline of sales forces.
- For advertising agencies – as manufacturers' advertising budgets are squeezed, retail advertising should grow. There will be more information for evaluation but also a necessity for speedier responses.
- For market research – more complex data, quicker, cheaper

test marketing. In the USA and France, TV commercials are tested directly, via CABLE TV, on CONSUMER PANELS whose purchases are being recorded electronically.

Equal impact strategy. Scheduling a campaign on TV so that an equal number of TVRs is targeted for each region.

Establishing a shot. Film/TV term for the shot which sets the scene at the opening or start of a new sequence, establishing in the viewer's mind what the film is about, its ambiance, its mood – e.g. the nostalgic country scenes that began Hovis commercials.

Evaluation. Nobody knows whether Lord Leverhulme really did say, '50% of my advertising expenditure is wasted, but I don't

Advertising roles and measures of effect		
Direct/indirect scale of response	Expected measures behaviour	Attitudes
Direct		
Direct response	Orders, replies	
Seek information	Coupons, enquiries	
Relate to own needs, wants, desires	Purchasing	Attitude change Salience change
Recall satisfactions, reorder shortlist	Purchasing	Brand salience/ brand awareness
Modify attitudes		Attitude change User image change
Reinforce attitudes		(No change) Added value tests
Indirect		

Source: Jeremy Elliott, 'Campaign evaluation'.

Evaluation case-history: Zanussi's appliance of science

Until 1976, Zanussi was almost unknown to the British consumer, despite being Europe's largest manufacturer of white goods. After building a distributor network for Zanussi-branded products, the company embarked in 1980 on the 'Appliance of Science' TV campaign, in which unseen beings from a technically advanced planet applied their science to constructing and delivering to Earth the most advanced appliances in the universe.
  Annual U & A studies showed results.

	1979 %	1980 %	1981 %	1982 %	1983 %	1984 %
Zanussi						
Spontaneous brand awareness	8	20	20	27	33	39
Brand imagery:						
Technically advanced products	20	31	34	39	44	48
Reliable products	14	13	13	22	26	25
Reputation for quality products	12	9	12	18	23	22
Good value for money	10	9	12	14	18	17
One of the biggest companies	6	6	7	8	12	16
Sales index (1979 = 100)						
Zanussi	100	93	126	138	162	n/a
Total market	100	93	91	104	113	n/a

Source: Jeremy Elliott, 'Campaign evaluation'.

---

know which 50%', but if he did he was confessing that he had never come to grips with evaluating advertising.

Evaluation involves setting realistic targets, monitoring results, learning from them and repeating the cycle year after year. Techniques for doing this vary, depending on your view of how advertising works and how it is intended to work for the particular campaign being evaluated (see ROLE FOR ADVERTISING).

The evaluation process should begin at the same time as

planning the campaign, for this is the stage when the hypothesis of how the campaign will work is set up, when specific targets (which effects, among whom) have to be estimated, when ways to monitor the effects of the campaign should be set up.

A useful way to look at the relationship between advertising roles and measures of effect takes the direct/indirect scale of advertising roles and relates them to methods of evaluation.★ See also ATTITUDES/ATTITUDE RESEARCH, MARKET MODELLING, PRE-TESTING, RECALL TESTS, TRACKING STUDY.

There is another pitfall – what response is it realistic to expect? As Jeremy Elliott† points out: 'if the target is met, is that success, or was the target too low? Is failure really failure, or over-ambitious target-setting?' Even with DIRECT RESPONSE you have to rely on previous experience or trial and error. Advertising which aims primarily to reinforce existing attitudes is extremely difficult to evaluate.

Ex-factory sales. A term for the sales that a manufacturer makes to his immediate customers (e.g. distributors, wholesalers, retailers). The difference between what he sells ex-factory and what the consumer buys is what is in the 'pipeline' (e.g. retailers' warehouses, shelves in the stores, etc.).

Extended group. A GROUP DISCUSSION given more time and opportunity, in a more relaxed atmosphere, to encourage its members to explore beyond the conscious, rational level reached by most groups. Six respondents is the ideal number, according to Sampson,★ as they can work in three pairs or two trios. PROJECTIVE TECHNIQUES are used. The session, with breaks for refreshments, can last up to 7 hours and the group may be reconvened.

See also SENSITIVITY PANEL.

F

Facing matter. Advertisements booked, at special rates, to be placed opposite editorial matter, instead of taking their chance among pages of other ads at the front or back of the publication.

Fee. Alternative way in which ADVERTISING AGENCIES charge CLIENTS. It is now a more frequent basis for negotiating payment than the traditional COMMISSION. Fees have always been paid for work not covered by the commission.

Fieldwork. The part of the research programme in which the data are being collected from the sample. The quality of the final research depends a great deal on the efficiency and supervision of the fieldwork.

Financial advertising. Once an esoteric corner of the advertising industry, handled by specialist agencies who understood such

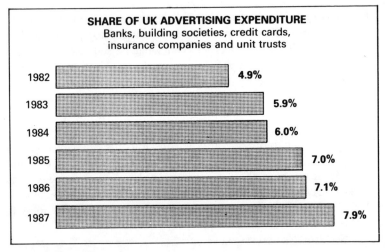

Source: MEAL, 1987

This diagram shows how advertising has become more important to the main financial institutions dealing with personal finance over the last six years. As the figures do not include the spending on the big privatization campaigns (such as Sid), their share of the advertising spend has grown even more dramatically.

things as company prospectuses, the Chairman's statement, what notices to AGMs or share issues had to contain, what a public company is obliged by law to make public.

Now the 'financial services industry' is a major advertiser, with individual banks, building societies, insurance companies and pension schemes all competing for the general public's money/savings/investments – not to mention the big privatization campaigns. In addition, the take-over battles spill over into the consumer-oriented press and TV advertising to win over shareholders (see CORPORATE ADVERTISING).

Financial advertising is controlled:

- By legislation such as the Consumer Credit Act and Regulations, and the Banking Act; the IBA lists 14 other Acts which are relevant.
- By a number of codes of practice: BCAP, the IBA CODE, and codes drawn up by the Building Societies, Banks and Finance Houses.

FMCG. Fast Moving Consumer Goods. The branded products on the monthly if not the weekly or daily shopping list, many now stocked by supermarkets. They sell fast (it is hoped); but attitudes towards them change very slowly.

Fount/Font. The complete set of all the letters, characters and figures, Roman and Italic, of one particular TYPEFACE in one size. 'Font' is the US spelling.

Frame. Single picture in a film sequence. There are 25 frames per second on TV film and 24 frames per second on cinema film.
    See STORYBOARD

Free offers. Also known as free premiums. They are given to you whether you want them or not. In-pack offers are inside the pack like plastic toys in breakfast cereals. Banded offers are attached to the pack, usually a sample of one of the manufacturer's other products. With-pack offers are given to purchasers of the pack at the point of sale, like the pioneering plastic daffodils.
    See also BELOW-THE-LINE.

Free sheets. Local free distribution publications financed by advertising and delivered free, usually door-to-door. A recent development made economic by new production technology. BRAD listed 1,039 titles in 1987; 140 were circulating in the Greater London area, one (the *Birmingham Daily News*) was appearing every weekday. Their share of total advertising revenue in 1987 was already outstripping that of paid-for weeklies. The circulations of some free sheets are now audited by VFD Ltd. (see ABC).

Frequency. The number of times the media schedule gives its target audience opportunities to see (OTS) or to hear (OTH). Can be applied to one particular commercial or an entire campaign.
    See EFFECTIVE COVERAGE/REACH, REPETITION.

Frequency distribution. Analysis to check what percentage of the target audience has had opportunities to see or hear the commercial or campaign once, twice or more often. It is frequently shown as follows:

OTS	1	2	3	4	5	0		
% target audience seeing	20	25	20	15	10	10	=	100

It's never easy, trying to come up with a Unique Award Winning Proposition

(Reprinted by kind permission of ADMAP)

Frequency of purchase. In each product field, the consumer's buying patterns vary. For FMCG, for example, the frequency of purchase may be once a week, but for a consumer durable, like a washing machine or freezer, it is (one hopes) at least several years before another needs to be purchased. Obviously, frequency of purchase directly affects the way a brand is advertised (see ROLE FOR ADVERTISING). Information comes from CONSUMER PANELS for frequently purchased goods, and *ad hoc* surveys for those bought less frequently.

Full-service agency. An ADVERTISING AGENCY which provides at the very least those services for CLIENTS which were originally paid for out of the COMMISSION. For example:

- ACCOUNT MANAGEMENT (see ACCOUNT DIRECTOR, ACCOUNT EXECUTIVE).
- Account planning/marketing/research advice (see ACCOUNT PLANNER).
- Creative work (see CREATIVE DEPARTMENT, CREATIVE TEAM, ART DIRECTOR, COPYWRITER, ART BUYER).
- Media planning and buying (see MEDIA PLANNER, MEDIA BUYER).
- PROGRESS (or traffic or control) DEPARTMENT to organize the progress of everything through the agency to the media.

Full service agencies also manage a lot of sub-contracted work that falls outside the commission and for which a FEE has always been negotiated, e.g.:

- Market research FIELDWORK.
- Finished ARTWORK – photography, illustrations, etc.
- TV, film and radio production.
- Design of PACKAGING, POINT OF SALE, devising PROMOTIONS – even when carried out by a specialist department within the agency.

G

Galley proof. The first proof submitted by the printer for initial reading and correction. Originally so called after the metal tray (the galley) used for the assembly of type before it is divided into its separate page formes. Copy is set in its correct column width but not in final pagination. With changes in typesetting technology, such as automatic page make-up systems, galley proofs are now seen less frequently.

Gatefold. A single page in a booklet or brochure which folds out to double its size. An example of its use is in multi-lingual instruction books, where the diagrams need only be printed once on the gatefold to be visible for every language section.

Generics. Products sold in plain packaging with no frills and no advertising. They are therefore basic and cheaper. The products are not quite commodities nor are they totally unbranded – they are perhaps more like PRIVATE LABEL goods. Early adopters of generics were the Carrefour hypermarkets who introduced their 'Produits Libres' and the Jewel Grocery chain in Chicago whose generics were only sold in Jewel stores. Although a generic corner can still be found in US stores, it is rare in the UK. Where the ultimate consumer has little or no control over brand choice, generics have been more successful as cheaper substitutes for brands. An example is the way generic unbranded drugs and medicines are used by the NHS.

Geodemographics. A method of classifying neighbourhoods and the households in them according to a wide range of demographic and social variables. This detailed on-ground information indicates where DIRECT MAIL should be addressed, where shops could most profitably be sited, where door-to-door is least wasteful, which poster sites to buy, which regional publications to advertise in, where to send the salesman, etc.

Various proprietary systems exist – e.g. ACORN, Pinpoint, Mosaic, Super Profile – all of which classify households using multi-variate analysis on the most recent census data. First to emerge in the 1970s was ACORN, using 40 variables developed from Richard Webber's work on urban deprivation.★ It identifies 11 different neighbourhood groups and is now also linked to the TGI.

More recent systems claim greater discrimination by using more variables – Super Profile uses 150, Pinpoint 104 – each arriving at its own dozen major classifications. They also claim greater accuracy: as direct mail depends on computer-matching addresses to the Census Enumeration Districts by means of the post-codes, Pinpoint's analysis, by computer mapping, of all post-code sectors in the UK and all enumeration district boundaries in London, and the corrections made as a result, are valuable.

Global advertising. An approach to international advertising and marketing, inspired by Theodore Levitt★ and taken up enthusiastically by Saatchis. The idea is 'world brands', marketed by multinationals, serviced by mega-agencies, using the same advertising material and commercials everywhere. This has the attractive corollary that production costs would be very much cheaper: only one world-wide campaign instead of separate creative work and TV commercials for each country.

There are, in the sense that they sell all over the world, many 'world brands' already, such as Coca Cola, Levi's jeans, Marlboro'. There are also many 'global' marketing companies, such as Unilever, Kodak, De Beers, Philips, Sony. But even companies like these do not impose the same advertising on every country (see INTERNATIONAL ADVERTISING, WORLD BRANDS). They would agree with the ex-Chairman of ICI: 'There is a cliché that the world is a single marketplace but the reality is that this is not true. Similar products are required but they have to be tailored and delivered to meet the national need . . . each of those markets requires a different response.'†

The world-wide communication networks and the promised advent of DBS are also supposedly forces for globalization. DBS is still struggling on the ground and the media empires (like Murdoch's) do not run the same editorial or programmes world wide. This suggests that even if space/time can be booked globally, it has to be filled locally.

Glossies. Magazines printed on glossy art paper which gives high quality reproduction for colour photography. This process is expensive, and therefore only used for UP-MARKET publications with a high cover price, such as *Harpers & Queen* and *Vogue*.

Government publications. Everything emanating from HMSO. No advertising permitted. Statistical publications such as *Monthly Digest of Statistics, Social Trends* or the Family Expenditure Surveys are all invaluable for desk research. All Acts of Parliament, White Papers, Green Papers, etc. are government publications.

Gravure. An intaglio printing process: the image to be printed is etched or sunk below the surface (the opposite of letterpress where the image is raised) and the recesses are filled with ink.

Rotogravure is the high-speed gravure process used for printing newspaper colour supplements, women's magazines and much packaging and is an economical process for long runs on cheap paper.

Photogravure is the photographic process for preparing the plates for gravure printing processes.

Group discussions. Basic and widely used technique for QUALITA-TIVE RESEARCH. A small group – usually no more than eight members of a TARGET GROUP – discusses a topic relevant to the brand or product field, such as entertaining for a client in the drink business. Each group session lasts between 1 and 3 hours, occasionally as little as half an hour. Discussion is unobtrusively chaired by an experienced group leader/interviewer.

The aim is to get the members of the group interacting with each other in a stimulating way so that new ideas are thrown up and insights into social habits and individual reactions obtained. The results are stimulating for ACCOUNT PLANNERS and the

Coca Cola advertising, both its strategy and its creative approach, is initated at headquarters in Atlanta, Georgia. But there is an input from each country, backed by continuous research programmes, to allow for different tastes and aspirations as well as varying legal requirements. In recent years, the advertising preferred by South American teenagers links the product with outdoor activities such as football and beach life while those in the UK respond more to images of Americana culled from films like American Graffitti. The ad shown here ran in the UK. With acknowledgements and thanks to Coca Cola GB and McCann-Erickson.

CREATIVE TEAM. They are also used to generate questions for later ATTITUDE and /or QUANTITATIVE RESEARCH.

Group discussions can be a quick, fairly cheap way to get instant reactions instantly reported in a superficial way, from a quickly-assembled group. At the other end of the spectrum, probing 'deeper' feelings in greater detail can be the result of meticulously planned interview guides, used on carefully-selected groups, run by experienced psychologists, taped, transcribed, subjected to full content analysis, reported in documents and presentations and related to other forms of research – which is expensive. Or anything in between.

Specialist market research companies arrange groups to a given specification and budget. They recruit people, provide the group leader/interviewer and the meeting place.

GRPs. Gross Rating Points – a term used in the USA for TVRS for TV campaigns or the total readership for each insertion in each publication in a press campaign.

Guard book. Agency records of all print ads produced for one particular client are traditionally kept in guard books, which have special guards on the binding edge to prevent the spine breaking as the book gets filled with VOUCHER COPIES.

Gutter. The unprinted margin on the page which allows for binding. Some publications will print over this margin, as well as the others.

See BLEED.

H

Half tone. See BLOCK

Hall test. Product test administered in a hall, or some other central location, rather than in people's homes. Easier to arrange and usually cheaper, but the disadvantage is that people are asked to try things out in an artificial context rather than the reality of their own homes.

Headline. (1) For the printer: the line of type at the top of the page separated from the text by a white space (also known as the 'running head'); (2) For the copywriter, as for the newspaper editor, it is one of the key elements in a press ad to lure the reader's attention. Many rules have been formulated about what constitutes a sure-fire headline. An early intelligent analysis was written by Claude Hopkins in 1923.* His advice, derived from coupon responses to mail-order ads, is still valid for DIRECT RESPONSE advertising. Subsequent READING AND NOTING research was also the basis for David Ogilvy's advice to his copywriters for creating headlines – appeal to self-interest, inject maximum news, include brand name, don't worry about length, never use tricky or irrelevant headlines; and use certain words either because they sell (e.g. AMAZING, NEW, FREE, NEVER BEFORE) or they select prospects (e.g. YOU, MOTHER, VARICOSE VEINS) or they have emotional impact (e.g. KISS, LOVE, MARRY, AFRAID, BABY, MONEY).

Heavy users. Consumers whose purchase of a brand or service is regular and above average. Can be valuable to identify them since, as a rough rule of thumb, in most product fields about one-quarter of users account for about three-quarters of the use of a brand.

Hierarchy of effects. The model of the way advertising works which assumes one stage follows another in a linear sequence. It is the basis for the CONVERSION MODELS such as AIDA and DAGMAR.

Honest. Third key word in BCAP (the others being LEGAL, DECENT and TRUTHFUL). It is intended to be understood in general terms – i.e. *no* advertisers should take advantage of people's credulity, vulnerability or lack of experience. More particularly it means

HOW TO WIN FRIENDS
AND INFLUENCE PEOPLE

"At 60 miles an hour the loudest noise in this new Rolls-Royce comes from the electric clock"

They Laughed When I Sat Down
At the Piano
But When I Started to Play!–

Three of the most famous headlines ever written, from the top: 1. Dale Carnegie's powerful promise, irresitable to millions. 2. Rolls-Royce – one of the headlines which made David Ogilvy famous. The sub-head continues the story: What makes Rolls-Royce the best car in the world? 'There is really no magic about it – it is merely patient attention to detail,' says an eminent Rolls-Royce engineer. 3. U.S. School of Music's successful enticement to sign up for thier correspondence course. (Quoted by Julian Watkins, 100 Great Advertisements, Dover Books 1959).

that 'the design and presentation of advertisements should be such as to allow each part of the advertiser's case to be easily grasped and clearly understood.' As every schoolboy knows, it is possible to be completely truthful but still, by omitting important information, not tell the truth. The requirement for honesty as well as truthfulness in advertising recognizes and tries to remedy this.

Hot shop/Third wave. Small 'creative' agencies which set themselves up (or were set up as satellites to big agencies) in New York in the 1960s were dubbed Hot Shops. Mary Wells, set up by Interpublic, was one of the first and was most famous for painting the Braniff Airlines' planes pink.

Third Wave is the collective noun for the most recent wave of 'hungry' and 'creative' small agencies which have been starting up in the UK.

Housewife. A doomed creature? In ad research, the one who began life as the wife of the male Head of the Household, who mainly stayed at home and looked after the family, the house, the cleaning, the cooking, fetching, carrying, arranging – and above all made most of the shopping decisions – may be a disappearing species, threatened by Working Women, House Husbands, Dinkies, Twinkies, Male Mums, *et al.* However, any one taking on the role of chief or joint shopper is of vital interest to advertisers and media owners.

The Mirror Group Newpapers began pointing out the husband's shopping role in 1973. In 1977 they wrote about 'Housepersons'. In 1986 they estimated there were 23.3 million housepersons of whom 3.6 million were men. Men are the sole housepersons in 2.4 million households. Since 1973, the number of households where 'the head and the houseperson are one and the same woman have risen by one-third to 5.8 million'.* The NRS now separates housewives into males and females.

Hypermarket. Supermarket with over 50,000 square feet of selling space.

Hypothetico-deductive methodology. A scientific methodology formulated by Popper and Medawar explaining the creative processes of scientific discovery, which seem to be as applicable at the humble level of advertising as at the heights of Nobel prizewinning science.

Its starting point is a hypothesis, derived from a scientific idea or intuition. This is then exposed to a logical series of rigorous tests and criticisms designed to disprove it. These are the experiments and observations of science which, contrary to tradition, do not come first. The hypothesis may survive all attempts at invalidation. If so, it can be accepted at a higher level of confidence. If not, it can be modified and the testing can begin afresh.

The relevance of this methodology to creating, planning and evaluating advertising has been most elegantly explored by Jeremy Bullmore. ★The creative idea, the intuition, the strategic idea are the hypotheses. The research, the criticism, the feedback are the rigorous attempts to invalidate or develop it. The result is a more fertile symbiosis between the creative and the marketing demands of advertising.

I bought it to complement our Mitsubishi TV, our Toshiba video, Fuji camera, Sanyo microwave, Hitachi cassette-player, Sony HiFi system, Yamaha synthesizer, Saisho cordless phone and Toyota estate car

(Reprinted by kind permission of ADMAP)

I

IBA. Independent Broadcasting Authority. The statutory body created by the 1954 Television Act to set up and supervise commercial television. Subsequent Acts (i.e. 1964 Television Act and 1981 Broadcasting Act) have strengthened and clarified its powers and added ILR (Independent Local Radio) to its responsibilities.

The IBA has three main areas of responsibility:

- To award contracts to the programme companies and monitor their performance (see ITV).
- To set up and maintain the transmitters for both ITV and ILR.
- To supervise the amount and content of the advertising.

Britain was the first country to set up commercial broadcasting, with strict separation of programme makers from the advertising interest, and to define this separation by law. An average of no more than six minutes of advertising per hour is allowed, and proposed advertising breaks are checked with each contractor when the programme schedules are set; programme sponsorship in the way it operates in the USA is *not* permitted.

The IBA also has a statutory duty to draw up and review a code of advertising practice (see IBA CODE OF ADVERTISING PRACTICE) in consultation with the Home Office. It can itself prohibit advertising contrary to its code, or relax it (as in the partial removal of the ban on contraceptive advertising in 1987). This role is carried out by the IBA's Advertising Advisory Committee.

In addition, the IBA has 'to secure compliance with the Code'. In this the ITV programme companies co-operate with the IBA by providing a secretariat which vets every script before production begins as well as checking the film before transmission.

IBA Code of Advertising Practice. Drawn up and revised in accordance with the 1954 and 1964 Television Acts, and the 1981 Broadcasting Act respectively. The IBA is not only obliged to create and enforce it, but also has the right to go beyond requirements of the code and exclude any advertising in general or particular circumstances. The ITV and ILR contractors are obliged to obey it. The code has the force of law behind it, but its day-to-day enforcement is the responsibility of the IBA which has the ultimate sanction that any contractor ignoring it, or accepting advertising which ignores it, can be deprived of his contract. General principles are, as in BCAP, that all advertising should be LEGAL, DECENT, HONEST and TRUTHFUL. But 'because of its greater intimacy within the home', special problems are recognized and the IBA Code spells out some rules in greater detail. For example:

- No ad 'should offend against good taste or decency or be offensive to public feeling'. The showing of WCs, nudes and near-nudes, etc., is controlled by what interpretation is put on this.
- No subliminal advertising, inertia selling or ads giving one side of a political or industrial controversy are permitted.
- Whole categories of goods and services cannot be advertised at all, e.g. religious organizations, 'unacceptable' products and services (which include breath-testing devices, fortune tellers, undertakers and, since 1965, cigarettes).
- Restrictions on all liquor advertising are stricter, e.g. it mustn't seem daring, masculine or sexy to drink, or acceptable habitually to drink alone.
- The ads must be separated from the programmes, so that they cannot be mistaken for part of the programme.

As in BCAP, all claims must be substantiated and testimonials must have consent. Any comparisons of one product with another must be fair 'with no likelihood of the consumer being misled'. Three Appendices define specific rules for advertising and children, financial advertising and the advertising of medicines and treatments.

Copies of the IBA Code are available from the IBA.

See also CHILDREN, CIGARETTES.

ILR. Independent Local Radio. The development of ILR mirrors that of ITV, except that coverage is still not national. Both function under the umbrella and control of IBA.

Each local station is a monopoly in its area – except in London where Capital Radio and LBC both transmit. The contracts are awarded on the basis of tenders submitted by approved groups who want, and show they can afford, to start up their local station and can persuade the IBA that they have appropriate programming plans. Following the 1973 Act, some 50 local radio stations now cover over 80 per cent of the UK population. On average, but this varies widely from station to station, they account for over 50 per cent of all radio listening.

The ILR is the section of the IBA which awards the contract, supervises and monitors the performance of each of its stations and the public's response. ILR also monitors the advertising. Time allowed is an average of 9 minutes per hour. Spots can be booked on one or two stations only or, as packages, over the whole network. Ads must keep within the IBA Code and the IBA has issued additional guidelines for radio. The content is checked and commercials are vetted at script stage. Finished commercials are monitored by ILR before transmission.

Impact. (1) Media term for one single exposure to an advertisement for one single person when OTS/OTH is judged to have been taken; (2) Loosely used for the overall effect of an ad – e.g. if it has been noticed at all (see PAGE TRAFFIC). Otherwise only subjective views are obtainable from small-scale QUALITATIVE RESEARCH.

Impression. Synonym for IMPACT in media terminology.

Impulse purchase. Something bought on the spur of the moment. Shops try to encourage it by attractive displays or irresistibly disordered ones strategically placed. It's no accident that sweets are so often temptingly within reach of the queue at the check-out.

Innovation. An intrinsic element of successful advertising. The number of second-hand ideas, ME-TOO brands and cut-price copies around indicate that this is not universally acknowledged or acted on. But the essence of an ADVERTISING IDEA is that, in some way, it is 'different'. The point of a BRAND PERSONALITY is that it is 'unique'. To create, in advertising, is to innovate – maybe quite superficially by using a new photographic or cinematic technique, or fundamentally by a completely new approach to an otherwise familiar and cliché-ridden subject.

New brands too need a degree of innovation. Analyses of their success/failure rate indicate that an essential component for success is that they should be 'better and different'.★

See also BRAND, NPD.

Insert. Advertising material which is designed to be delivered with and inside a publication. Bound-in inserts are bound into the publication, tip-ins are slipped in loose.

International advertising. Until the concept of GLOBAL ADVERTIS-ING arrived, international advertising was either what multi-nationals were doing, or what a manufacturer building up his exports abroad did. The multinationals, with offices or sub-sidiaries around the world, tended to use agencies with interna-tional networks. In fact the American agencies began establishing their bridgeheads in Europe in the 1920s just to service American companies – e.g. in 1923 the JWT London office opened to handle the General Motors account. Many successful WORLD BRANDS have developed recognizable, but not identical cam-paigns, in their various markets. Each culture has its own different values and symbols which mean brands are accepted in different ways – the Pepsi generation campaign which started off in the USA for the generation of young Americans who were bright, clean and scrubbed and played volleyball on the beach, took on broader associations from anti-establishment rebellion to growing out of childhood elsewhere in the world.★

For the manufacturer entering a 'foreign market' the situation is rather different and described as 'a minefield for the unwary . . . at best . . . exactly the same as advertising at home only even more difficult'.† Languages, cultures and customs vary, as do regulations about what can be advertised and how; in Europe alone the amount of time allowed for TV commercials varies from none at all in Denmark, Norway and Sweden to 40 minutes a day in West Germany and 2 hours 20 minutes a day in the UK.

In developed countries there is a choice between using one of the international agencies who have offices there, or local agencies. Elsewhere these are few and far between, or non-existent.

Information is sometimes difficult to come by. The Interna-tional Advertising Association publishes a *Guide to International*

Markets with basic details and individual data sources for 100 countries. The IPA publishes a series of guides to conditions in various markets. *Advertiser's Annual* and *Advertising Age* both publish useful, but not exhaustive, lists of media, billings and agencies annually.

Interviewer card scheme. Scheme started by Market Research Society in 1978 so that the general public can identify interviewers who are conducting genuine surveys. Since 1987 bona fide interviewers have carried the Interview Identity Card. But everyone still has the right to refuse to be interviewed whether the interviewer produces this card or not.

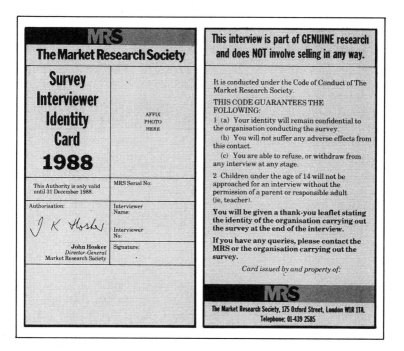

The 1988 Interviewer Identity Card issued by the MRS. Each interviewer has his or her own card with their photograph on it. On the reverse side the MRS code is spelt out so as to guarantee the research is genuine. With acknowledgements and thanks to the Market Research Society.

IPA. Institute of Practioners in Advertising. The advertising agencies' trade association, its industry spokesman and information centre. It began life in 1917 as the Association of British Advertising Agents, and re-formed as IPA in the 1920s. Over 300 agencies are members – out of an estimated total of over 1,000 – but IPA agencies account for over 90 per cent of advertising placed through agencies.

Would-be members must satisfy the IPA of their professional capacity (normally a staff of no less than six and a turnover in excess of £1 million), and their willingness to uphold ethical standards and industry codes. They must also provide 'recognition' (of their credit-worthiness) from at least two of the three main media bodies.

The IPA has been active in promoting research into media and instrumental in forming Joint Industry Committees – e.g. JICNARS, the Joint Industry Committee for National Readership Surveys (see NRS). There are similar committees for radio (JICRARS), posters (JICPAR) and cable (JICCAR). For TV, IPA represents the agencies on the Audience Measurement Committee of BARB. In 1980, in order to demonstrate the measurable commercial effectiveness of advertising, the IPA established the biennial ADVERTISING EFFECTIVENESS AWARDS competition. The IPA's series of education and training programmes – 'The 7 Stages' – are short intensive courses catering for the training needs of members' employees at critical stages of their careers. These range from evening series for trainees to breakfast symposia for senior management. For professional exams and qualifications see CAM.

ISBA. Incorporated Society of British Advertisers. The advertisers' trade association to which most major advertisers belong. While actively co-operating with other national and international advertising groups (e.g. the AA, IPA, CBI) it also aims to enable advertisers to speak with one voice. It represents their views on advertising matters to the government, opinion leaders, media owners, advertising agencies and the public. A view it works to establish is that advertisers should have freedom to advertise their goods and services in all media, subject only to the law, the

Codes and well-established editorial policy. It promotes and supports high standards of advertising practice.

Its work is carried out through a series of committees, each specializing in one topic – e.g. exhibitions, press advertising, research, sales promotion. ISBA publishes newsletters, guides and pamphlets, among them *Guide to Direct Mail, Choosing an Advertising Agency, Value Analysis in Advertising*. It also runs an information service, conferences, seminars and workshops.

ITVA. Independent Television Association. The trade association for ITV programme companies. There are 16 ITV companies which hold contracts awarded by the IBA. Fifteen transmit programmes on a regional basis. They are: Anglia, Border, Central, Channel, Grampian, Granada, HTV, London Weekend, Scottish, TSW (Television South West), TVS (Television South), Thames, Tyne Tees, Ulster, Yorkshire. TV-am provides ITV's national breakfast service. Channel 4 is a wholly-owned subsidiary of the IBA, but it is financed by subscriptions from the ITV companies who in return sell its advertising time.

ITVA carries out the necessary checks of the advertising and the administration of the IBA CODE on behalf of Channel 4 and the ILR companies as well as all the ITV companies. The Copy Clearance Department checks all scripts before production. Each year some 16,000 TV and 11,000 radio advertisement scripts are submitted, most of which are cleared by the Copy Secretariat without further discussion. Every completed TV commercial is also seen by the Advertising Control Department of the IBA.

ITVA produces Notes of Guidance which are described as 'the creative advertising person's working textbook on how to produce an effective advertisement without breaking any of the rules'.

BARB is jointly owned by the BBC and ITVA.

ITV. Independent Television. All TV under the aegis of the IBA. Programme listings call the original channel ITV to distinguish it from Channel 4 and TV-am.

See IBA, ITVA.

J

Jingle. The catchy little song about the product forming all or part of a sound track. Specialists in the genre are commissioned to write words and music, and orchestrate and record them. They get a royalty every time the commercial runs on TV or is shown in the cinema.

Junk mail. DIRECT MAIL perceived as irrelevant. Typical examples are those personally-addressed letters estate agents send to your teenagers, begging to be allowed to sell the family home to one of a long list of diplomats queuing to pay cash.

Justify. To arrange the words and spaces making up each line of type so that both margins are aligned vertically. Unjustified text has one margin (usually the left) aligned but not the other.

K

Key fact. Part of some CREATIVE BRIEFS. A single-minded statement that sorts out, from all the information about product market, competition, etc., the element that is most relevant to advertising.

Knocking copy. COMPARATIVE ADVERTISING that goes too far. At one time 'not done', but today some slips through (see BCAP).

L

Laser printing. Lasers are used in new print technology for photosetting, colour scanning, copy scanning, platemaking and engraving. For printing the image is created by a laser being switched on and off according to digital information controlled by a computer.

Lateral thinking. Edward de Bono★ coined this term to describe a way of thinking different from the step-by-step, logical and deductive thought processes within which most people are accustomed to working. He invents techniques to interrupt and break up the straight and narrow deductive flow with random stimuli, deliberate challenges to hitherto agreed principles and introducing what he terms 'the intermediate impossible'. The aim is to jolt thought processes sideways (laterally) to open up original, unexpected, creative solutions. Many find his ideas very relevant to solving advertising problems and getting ADVERTISING IDEAS.

See also HYPOTHETICO–DEDUCTIVE METHODOLOGY.

Layout. (1) Design for print ads, for example, to show how an idea will work out in practice in the planned space. The type of illustration, headline, copy length, captions, logos and sign–offs are all indicated, but the finish varies from ROUGH to enough detail to show to the CLIENT. Only after client approval is ARTWORK commissioned and typography worked out. (2) Specifically the typographer's contribution – the layout with type faces and sizes marked out. These are the printer's instructions for setting (See TYPE, TYPEFACE).

Legal. First key word in BCAP – followed by DECENT, HONEST and TRUTHFUL. Advertisements must not contain anything in breach of the law, nor omit anything the law requires. Nor must they contain anything likely to bring the law into disrepute.

BCAP is self-regulatory (see ASA). The IBA has Statutory powers to regulate its code. In addition there is a formidable body of statute law and common law which affects advertising. The 1981 IBA code lists a selection of 46 General Statutes and 16

Financial Acts which it says 'should be particularly noted'. Of particular importance to any advertiser are:

- The Trade Descriptions Act 1968 which controls how goods and services are described.
- The Medicines Act 1986 (and regulations under it) whereby advertisements for medicines must conform to the terms of a licence issued by the Medicines Commission for each product.
- The Fair Trading Act 1973.
- The Food and Drugs Act 1955 (as amended) which contains requirements for the advertising and labelling of food.
- The Consumer Credit Act 1974, governing form and content of credit advertising.

See IBA CODE OF ADVERTISING PRACTICE.

Letterpress. Printing from a raised surface. A technique known to the Chinese in the sixth century AD. In Western Europe Gutenberg's breakthroughs, around 1440, were his invention of movable cast metal type, which was gripped in a wood forme, and ink of the right viscosity to print clearly on to the paper. London's first press was founded by William Caxton in 1475, and most printing was done by letterpress until 100 years ago. Today it still has the advantage of producing a crisp image, but photosetting has to a great extent replaced the hot metal and/or plastic at both small printers and the national newspapers.

Life stages. DEMOGRAPHIC classifications linked to major changes in people's lives rather than the universal standard age categories. For example:

- Finding a regular partner.
- Getting married/setting up home.
- Arrival of first child/loss of one income.
- Youngest child starts school/possibility of second income.
- Last child leaves home/empty nest.
- Retirement.

These changes are considered to affect attitudes, disposable income and behaviour much more dramatically than age change *per se.* See SOCIO-ECONOMIC CLASSIFICATIONS.

SAGACITY GROUPINGS

Sagacity, developed by Research Services Ltd is an example of a classification system based on life stages, assuming that people's aspirations and behaviour patterns change as they go through their life cycle.

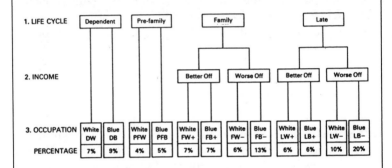

The above distribution is based on NRS data for the first six months of 1986

Sagacity identifies four main life stages:

The Dependent Stage: informants are still living within their family or studying full-time if living away from home.

The Pre-family Stage: adults under 35 yrs old who have established their own households, but as yet have no children.

The Family Stage: all households (whose heads are under 65) with one or more children under 21 living at home.

The Late Stage: all adults whose children have left home or who are over 35 and childless.

Two further subdivisions are made. One is based on income and divides people in the Family and the Late Stages into the Better Off and Worse Off.

The second is based on occupation of informant's head of household: white collar covers ABC1, blue collar C2DE (see SOCIO-ECONOMIC GROUPS).

So FW + means: F = family stage, W = white collar work, + = better off.

Percentages of people in each classification are marked on the diagram. The numbers are based on NRS data.

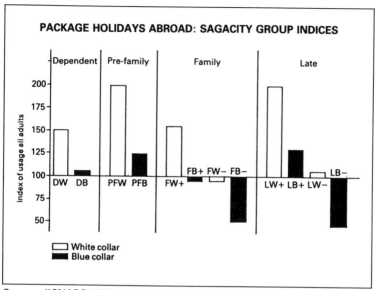

Source: JICNARS 1980

An example from Research Services Ltd of the kind of insight into the way a market is influenced by age and life cycle that classification like Sagacity can give.

Lifestyles. PSYCHOGRAPHICS which have been specially developed for advertisers and media owners are generally packaged and marketed as 'lifestyles'. All base their data on long questionnaires and large samples, giving opportunities for statistical analysis, novel clustering, etc.

Leo Burnett's first 'Life Style Research' (early 1970s) was based on an initial sample of 10,000 and a questionnaire asking for agree/disagree ratings (see ATTITUDE/ATTITUDE RESEARCH) on as many as 230 'Life Style' statements ranging from 'Trade Unions come in for a lot of unfair criticism' to 'I love feeling fur.' It divided men into 7 clusters and women into 6, each enlivened by some descriptions: 'He's young, got money to spend. Andy seeks his pleasures quite selfishly and has few moral scruples. He's educated and ambitious in his job. Up grade.' As with all CLUSTER ANALYSIS, such vivid descriptions of the stereotyped

123

individual can be slightly misleading: e.g. 65 per cent of Andys had not continued their education beyond the age of 16, as against 73 per cent of all men; 38 per cent claimed their job was boring (32 per cent of all men).*

RBL's Panel Project (1972) worked on a smaller, simpler scale, mixing traditional background classifications with general values and attitudes, interests and leisure activities, husband/wife role relationships and the purchase of 20 new products. They came up with 8 attitudinal clusters to which they gave original names like 'the Young Sophisticates', 'Cabbages' ('Mrs Cabbage lives a very sheltered life') and 'Coronation Street housewives'.†

In 1987 a new system, Outlook, took 192 attitudinal statements from the 1985/86 TGI, together with information on media viewed or read, brand and product use. It came up with 6 new 'Lifestyle' clusters: 'Trendies', 'Pleasure seekers', 'the Indifferent', 'Working class puritans', 'Social spenders', 'Moralists' (who are against everything enjoyable, except gardening).‡

Lip sync. Synchronizing a film's sound track with the visual, so that the movements of the artiste's lips match what is being said.

List broker. Specialist who collects and puts together mailing lists from various sources (see DIRECT MAIL).

Litho. Lithography. Printing from a flat surface, based on the principle that oil and water do not mix. The printing plate was originally a limestone block and the inks were oil-based, so the area to be printed was treated with fatty oils, the rest damped with water. This method is still used by artists. Commercially, the process today is virtually all 'offset lithography' by which the plate never comes into contact with the paper. The positive image from the plate (now metal) is transferred onto a rubber 'blanket' and becomes a negative, then is transferred again, as a positive image, onto the paper (see WEB–OFFSET).

Photolitho is the process for making the litho plates photographically. The image is transferred on to a sensitized zinc or aluminium plate which is then developed so as to leave a water-sensitive surface on the non–image areas.

Live action. Scenes filmed as they happen with live artistes – the actors, dogs, babies, cars, etc. – just as in feature films. As opposed to ANIMATION, STOP FRAME.

Locals. Regional daily and weekly newpapers selling or delivered free in one locality or region. Some are independent, most are part of a larger group; some very parochial, some (like the *Yorkshire Post*) influential over a whole region. Many are listed in BRAD with ABC circulation figures.

Logo. Originally the trade mark, now the way a BRAND or a company's name is written or symbolized, or the way it is incorporated into a sign-off formula or slogan at the foot of an ad. The style adopted becomes an element in the emotional appeal of a brand.
See CORPORATE LOGO.

Lower case. Small letters of the alphabet as opposed to capitals which are also referred to as 'upper case'.

Lucied layout. A mechanical working layout, on layout paper, to give the printer all the necessary working details for printing. It specifies the exact size and positioning of all illustrations and typematter, the typefaces (sizes, leading, spacing) and, if letterpress blocks are required, gives block tracings. Lucied Layout machines enable tracings in all the sizes necessary for a range of different publications to be made from the original layout.

M

Magazines/ Consumer publications. Many and varied, covering every aspect of life. Think of the serried ranks of weeklies, bi-weeklies, monthlies, quarterlies, annuals, etc., on view at every newsagent. Production and quality vary from art-directed GLOSSIES to no-frills weeklies like the *The Spectator*. Readership/ circulations also vary from mass-market (*Woman, Woman's Own*) to highly specialized readerships (*Custom Car, The Herbal Review*). Many are covered by NRS. Very precise targeting is possible to reach particular TARGET GROUPS via this medium.

Mail order. A method of distribution through the post – an alternative to opening a shop or selling to a retailer – which is becoming increasingly popular. The big mail order catalogues (e.g. Littlewoods) have been joined by growing numbers of 'Off-the-page' houses (e.g. Scotcade).

The buyer orders from an advertisement, from a mailing shot or from a catalogue. The goods are sent within a specified time limit. Payment can be by credit card. It has many advantages for both buyer and seller; for the former there is only the disadvantage of being at the mercy of the Post Office, if used, for charges and delivery.

The buyer is now protected from the worst sharks by codes of practice.

• BCAP specifies that descriptions must be accurate, sets out customers' rights to refunds, deliveries on time, etc. It also puts the onus for making sure goods are as described and that companies advertising have the financial resources to supply and deliver them, on the media in which the ads appear. So the media owners, through the NPA, THE NEWSPAPER SOCIETY and the PPA, for instance, run their own mail order protection schemes. (MOPS).
• The Mail Order Transactions (Information) Order 1976 requires advertisers to put their full name and address on any advertising.
• The Consumer Credit (Advertisement and Quotations) Regulations 1980 requires that offers of credit must show repayment terms in full including APR (the Annual Percentage Rate of Charge).

See DIRECT RESPONSE.

Mailing. Distribution of the DIRECT MAIL shot.

Mandatories. Client and legal restrictions and requirements as to content of advertising – e.g. inclusion or exclusion of particular words, phrases, logos, copyright marks.

Market map. A graphical representation of how brands relate to each other in a market. The simplest sort comes from setting two bi-polar scales, representing the key dimensions in the market, at right angles to each other, which is a very helpful way to show or

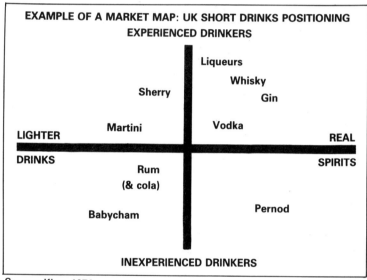

EXAMPLE OF A MARKET MAP: UK SHORT DRINKS POSITIONING
EXPERIENCED DRINKERS

Liqueurs
Whisky
Gin
Sherry
Martini
Vodka
LIGHTER
DRINKS
REAL
SPIRITS
Rum
(& cola)
Babycham
Pernod
INEXPERIENCED DRINKERS

Source: King, 1970

This is a notional market map for short drinks. Relative positions are plotted in the appropriate segments – in this case the two criteria are experienced/inexperienced drinkers and lighter drinks/real spirits. Actual placings arise out of what is known about consumers' drinking patterns. The significance of each section is judged from current market trends. It is one thing from a 'map' of this sort to see a gap in the market, but another to judge whether there is a market in the gap. Where, for instance, would one ideally position a new brand of ready-mixed Kir?

diagnose BRAND POSITIONING. Then ATTITUDE RESEARCH is used to plot consumers' perceptions of each brand on the map. It is of course possible to construct a conceptual map, using more than two dimensions. But we are used to two-dimensional maps, and what more elaborate mapping gains in richness it tends to lose in over-complication.

Market modelling. Making a model (or representation) of how a market works – what are the influences on it, what is their relative importance, how they interact. Increasingly today this involves ECONOMETRIC methods, the use of which has been boosted by recent developments in computer software. These methods make it possible to represent how a market works in mathematical terms. So the effects of variables (advertising expenditure, price changes, the weather, disposable income, etc. and their relationship to each other) can be expressed statistically. The big advantage is that many more variables including the all-important time variable can be accommodated and investigated. Problems do arise from the difficulties in translating each variable into a sufficiently accurate figure.

Market modelling is an important tool in many ways:

- For understanding how markets work and consumer buying patterns within them.
- For setting marketing and advertising budgets.
- For projecting effects of changes to marketing mix or new strategies.
- For evaluating advertising effectiveness and the return on investment of advertising and other promotional expenditure.

Market research. The definition in the Market Research Society's Code of Conduct has been (since November 1986): 'the collection and analysis of data from a sample of individuals or organisations relating to their characteristics, behaviour, attitudes, opinions, or possessions. It includes all forms of marketing and social research such as consumer and industrial surveys, psychological investigations, observational and panel studies.' In other words, the collection of primary data via field research. This is carried out by specialist market research companies, who in turn specialize in the type of research they organize; some of these are subsidiaries of ADVERTISING AGENCIES, most are not (see MRS).

Often market research has a broader meaning, including:

● Desk research – the collection of secondary data from published information such as directories, Government statistics, lists, past surveys, etc.
● Market intelligence – gathering of information from any outside sources that may contribute to a marketing plan. This general information gathering is done both within agencies (e.g. by ACCOUNT EXECUTIVES, ACCOUNT PLANNERS) and companies (e.g. by BRAND MANAGERS), or it can be bought from specialists such as Mintel.

"Sir Terence has found this gap in the market for couples who live in sin"

(Reprinted by kind permission of ADMAP)

Market segmentation. The theory that consumers in any market can be divided into discrete sub-groups (or segments) which have identifiably different patterns of needs, wants and desires. If the marketing company can identify the segments whose desires accurately match what its brand has to offer, then the marketing and advertising can be concentrated on them – clearly far more efficient than aiming at the population as a whole. Niche marketing is the term for very precisely focussed market segmentation.

However, there are many slips between theory and practice. Segmentation does work for product types – owners of fully automatic washing machines buy low-suds detergents; women (mostly) buy cosmetics; parents of small children buy tricycles – but there is little evidence that it works for BRANDS: though Persil and Ariel are very different brands, there is no significant segment of consumers that buys each exclusively. Most people have a REPERTOIRE of brands from which they choose. At best, there exists a mild tendency towards market segmentation for brands.

Even when we've identified a segment of consumers of particular interest, we usually find that their use of media is not very different from that of the population in general. So, although we can optimize our media selection, we cannot normally direct advertising exclusively at our chosen segment. The unsatisfactory results of using DEMOGRAPHICS for segmenting markets has led people to explore more sophisticated measures such as LIFESTYLES or PSYCHOGRAPHICS. VALS (Values, Attitudes and Lifestyles) was devised by the Stanford Research Institute to classify consumers by expressed social values and attitudes, and has been taken up by Young & Rubicam to apply to advertising. But such broadly-based and fundamental divisions of people as VALS are really too heavy-weight to deal with the relative triviality of people's choice between brands. As John Jones★ shows: 'Standardised brand penetration data shows that . . . important competitive brands are all used in the main by the same types of people, with only differences of emphasis in the importance of various demographic and psychographic groups . . . and as brands grow . . . as a result of growth of their user base . . . the overlap with other brands becomes greater because of the increase of multi-brand purchasing.'★

Market share. Proportion of defined market held by a BRAND, expressed in percentages.

Marketing mix. The elements that make up the total marketing process, of which the advertising is just one part. The mix includes:

- The product, and the way the product might be developed;
- its price – discounts, response to competitors' price policy, trade mark-ups;
- its distribution, from warehousing, sales force to ultimate selling point;
- its promotion, which includes BELOW-THE-LINE promotions and merchandising as well as PR and ABOVE-THE-LINE advertising.

The BRIEF is the Client's definition of the role the advertising should play within the marketing mix.

Marketing myopia. Famous Theodore Levitt★ concept in which he diagnosed one cause of certain companies' marketing failure. He found these were companies who classified the business they were in by what they produced rather than by what consumer wants they met. His memorable example was the US Railroad companies – a declining industry, he said, which limited itself to rail travel when it should have been thinking 'Transportation', and presumably gone into airlines, Greyhound buses or even set up in competition to Ford.

Its significance lies in being one of the first marketing hypotheses to point out the need to look at markets from the consumer's point of view as well as the producer's.

Married print. The stage in film-processing after the DOUBLE HEAD – the visual and the sound track have been 'married' on to a single negative. Changes of mind not advisable now.

Me-too. The fatal enemy of INNOVATION. All too many new products fail through copying a successful idea and imitating not only the product but its packaging and presentation. The public is not fooled by me-too advertising. The sophisticated CONSUMER recognizes it and tends to respond by discounting it.

MEAL. Media Expenditure Analysis Ltd. An independent information service which monitors advertising expenditure. Figures assume mid–ratecard rates have been paid. Analysis is done monthly, by region, by product, etc., in the press, on TV and on radio (not cinema or posters) and so indicates what the competition is spending in those media.

Media. In the advertising world, anything in or on which space or time for an ad can be booked, from TV to T-shirts, posters to parking meters.

The inter-media decision is which media (press, TV, radio) to use. The intra-media decision is which national newspaper, which TV or radio area.

Media buyer. Agency person (or independent: see MEDIA INDEPENDENT) who actually negotiates to buy the space/time, who in small agencies often doubles as MEDIA PLANNER. The area is very competitive, as for published media the rates shown on the RATE CARDS are negotiable, and for TV rates are very complex (see PRE-EMPT). At the end of each campaign, the media buyer has to prove to his client that his schedule has achieved value for money. Some advertisers check this for themselves independently, or employ specialists to do it for them.

And this is Doctor Mesmer, our expert in Aided Recall

(Reprinted by kind permission of ADMAP)

Media independent. Specialist MEDIA PLANNERS and MEDIA BUYERS. They offer a media-only service. Their numbers and the amount of business they handle have grown explosively since the late 1960s when the first ones were set up: there are now about 50 in the UK and they are reckoned to handle between 15 and 20 per cent of all media bookings, and even work alongside media departments of established agencies. The same phenomenon is happening to a greater or lesser extent throughout Europe and the USA. As they have much lower overheads than the FULL SERVICE AGENCIES, media independents can operate on a far lower rate of COMMISSION, which cuts costs for both advertisers and the agencies using them.

Before any space/time can be booked, all media independents have to get 'recognition' from the relevant media trade associations – such as the ITVA, the NPA, the PPA, etc. – who have to be satisfied about their professional reputations, their financial stability and their commitment to supporting the industry's various codes of practice.

Media planner. The media planner has an important role at the planning stage of a campaign when the whole ACCOUNT GROUP works together to define the TARGET GROUP and decide on the creative approach. These, and the overall budget, affect the inter-media decision – whether to use press, TV, posters or radio or a mix.

The media planner's responsibility is the intra-media selection. If press – which magazines or newspapers. If TV – what time of day, which regions. If posters – which sites. If radio – which spots. As media research has generated avalanches of statistics on readership, coverage, frequency, etc., target audiences for each medium are defined in detail, but in terms which seldom match the agency's target group in detail; only a few databases link media research with consumer living and buying habits. Building a media schedule is sometimes like squaring the circle (see BARB, NRS, PROFILE, TGI).

A media planner needs analytic skills, in contrast to a media buyer's social and bargaining skills. Most work in agencies. Planners in MEDIA INDEPENDENTS are at a disadvantage if they are not in close symbiotic contact with an account group or a CREATIVE TEAM.

Merchandising. Everything that can be done in-store to feature the product or service and make it irresistible at the point of sale. Merchandising activity can range from providing a little display unit for the counter, a shelf-wobbler or a show card saying 'As seen on TV' to taking over and fitting up part of a big store for particular BRANDS. Successful merchandising depends a great deal on the retailer. The big MULTIPLES, for instance, have strict controls over what brand owners may do. The most effective merchandising is planned, timed and carried out to complement any advertising campaign or BELOW-THE-LINE activity.

Metaphor. The Marlboro' cowboy, the Esso tiger and the Andrex puppy are examples of the power of metaphor when imaginatively used for advertising. A metaphor can dramatize a straightforward product claim – the Esso tiger can be seen as metophor for 'gives extra power/acceleration to your car'.

But, perhaps more important, it is a very effective way to build up a BRAND PERSONALITY; the tiger is a metaphor for a sleek, smooth, powerful, feline brand. The cowboy – a rugged,

The Andrex puppy. With acknowledgements and thanks to Scott Limited and the J. Walter Thompson Company Limited. Photo Keith Pettinato.

The Esso tiger. With acknowledgements and thanks to Esso Petroleum Company, Limited and McCann-Erickson.

individualistic, mythical male in tune with the great outdoors – is a powerful personality to give to a strong, uncompromising cigarette. The puppy is a soft, lovable member of the family.

Many campaigns aiming at an indirect response (see ROLE FOR ADVERTISING) succeed in creating interest through a vivid metaphor. Bernstein★ calls it 'poetic truth', and metaphor in advertising, as in poetry, makes the reader/viewer see freshly something he may previously have regarded as commonplace.

Motivation research. Research, usually small-scale, which aims to uncover reasons for consumer behaviour – motives and feelings, often concealed or irrational, which could affect the purchase and use of products and services. Its use for advertising was first proselytized in the USA during the 1950s by Dr Ernst Dichter.

But 'motives', whether the basic drives (sex, hunger, etc.) or social secondary drives (desire to possess, to control, to be social, to be held in high regard, to help, etc.) are now perceived as only one of the variables affecting the way consumers behave in the market place. It is more a matter of the way people's attitudes, motives and personality traits interact with external factors like product performance, availability and price. See ATTITUDE RESEARCH, DEPTH INTERVIEWS, GROUP DISCUSSIONS, PROJECTIVE TECHNIQUES, QUALITATIVE RESEARCH, SENSITIVITY PANEL.

MRS. Market Research Society. Founded in 1946, the MRS is the incorporated professional body in the UK for those using survey techniques for market, social and economic research. It aims to promote professional standards; it has drawn up a Code of Conduct and, among other things, initiated the INTERVIEWER CARD SCHEME. It provides a focus for discussion through its publications, seminars and conferences. In 1987 there were over 5,500 individual members. ESOMAR (European Society for Opinion and Market Research) is the international professional body.

Multiples. A retail organization with 10 or more outlets is known as a multiple.

The growth of multiples at the expense of independent stores (and to a slightly lesser extent, co-ops) has been one of the most important factors affecting the marketing of FMCG in the UK over the last 25 years. Multiple retailers have led the way in their investment in self-service and premises, which has resulted in the creation of ever-larger stores (see HYPERMARKETS, SUPERSTORES).

One key to their growth was the ending of RPM (in 1964), which allowed them to use their buying power to put price pressure on manufacturers and offer lower prices to consumers. This increased their profits, so they grew larger, increasing their buying power further, etc., into a 'virtuous spiral'. Manufacturers' advertising expenditures were affected as they felt obliged to pour more of their marketing budgets into price cutting and promotions. The big manufacturer brands have kept up their advertising expenditures and with that their market shares and profits, but the middle-sized brands have been severely squeezed between the brand leaders and the PRIVATE LABEL.

N

Names/Naming. The name is part of a successful BRAND PERSONALITY, but its role is not always the same for every brand (see BRAND NAME). There are no rules for how to go about generating a new winner. It's an exercise in LATERAL THINKING, associations and inspiration. Sometimes BRAINSTORMING sessions are used. Like new clothes, new names have to be tried for size – the early work on Yorkie, for example, was done under the names of 'Rations' and 'Trek'.

Nationals. Newspapers which sell throughout the UK. Categorized by BRAD into national daily newspapers (16), Sunday newspapers (22). Increasing numbers now have colour supplements.

Nationals are further subdivided informally into:

- The populars or TABLOIDS with mass-market circulations, e.g. the *Sun* which is now selling nearly 4 million copies daily.
- The mid-market papers such as the *Daily Express* and *Daily Mail* (also tabloids) which vie with each other at under 2 million copies daily.
- The quality press of which only the *Daily Telegraph* is currently selling more than 1 million copies daily. This category includes the *Financial Times,* the *Guardian,* the *Independent, The Times,* and on Sundays, the *Observer,* the *Sunday Telegraph* and the *Sunday Times.*

In spite of increasing competition from TV and radio, the combined circulations of nationals remain very constant: in 1960 116 million copies were sold each week, in 1984 the number was 109 million – a drop of only 6 per cent. Fortunes of individual titles have varied quite dramatically: in that period we have seen the demise of the *Herald,* the rise of the *Sun,* the launch of the *Independent,* and the slowly declining circulations of the *Daily Mirror, Daily Express* and *Daily Mail.*

Net homes. Areas served by different TV contractors overlap, e.g. many homes in the TVS area can also get programmes from Thames and LWT. When calculating the total number of homes where a particular commercial/campaign could be seen, this 'overlap' must be taken into account. 'Net homes' is the number of homes after allowance for 'overlap' has been made.

Network. Sociological concept dealing with the areas in which people's lives interact – family, children, school, business/work, neighbourhoods, relations. Many of its ideas, such as opinion leader, gatekeeper, peer group, have been borrowed from academic work in communications, e.g. the works of Klapper; Katz and Lazarsfeld; Hovland, Janis and Kelly. It is relevant for advertising because trends are built up through network influence. Healthy eating, entertaining, alcohol intake, whether you rely on family, friends or neighbours, are examples of this. Also, networks are the channels for word-of-mouth advertising, the value of which is acknowledged but impossible to measure.

New business pitch. ADVERTISING AGENCIES often have to compete with each other for new business, or even to keep old business if there is a new broom at the CLIENT end. This involves PRESENTATIONS. As a preliminary stage there is the Credentials Pitch. The agency discusses its philosophy, shows its work, introduces its most impressive people to the prospective client. The client sees a number of agencies and either decides on one there and then or, more often, makes a short list.

For most accounts of reasonable size, the client then calls for competitive pitches which involve the presentation of the proposed advertising strategy and, usually, new creative work. Several agencies will be briefed and may be provided with a fee to cover part of their often considerable costs. A strategy proposal may be impeccable, but clients' decisions are understandably swayed by their reactions to the creative work – hence the effort and expense agencies incur to make finished films and to print up advertisements.

The Newspaper Society. The association of regional (LOCAL) daily and weekly newspaper publishers for whom it performs a role similar to that of the NPA and the PPA for their members. Its activities affecting advertising include 'recognition' (with NPA, PPA etc.) of agencies; participation (with ASA) in formulating and administering BCAP as well as advising and keeping members informed about it; a mail order protection scheme (see DIRECT RESPONSE); vetting (also with NPA) ads for holidays and franchises.

NFS. National Food Survey. The basic source of information about food consumption in the British home. Seven thousand housepersons keep a diary of all the food bought and eaten, and by whom it is eaten, during one week, plus any expenditure on meals eaten out. Published annually, but some data available quarterly.

Neilsen. See RETAIL AUDITS.

NPA. Newspaper Publishers Association. Membership covers national daily and Sunday papers. Its activities which affect advertising include: advising members on BCAP; pre-vetting schemes for certain categories of ads such as franchises, holidays and home improvements; a mail order protection scheme (see DIRECT RESPONSE) co-operating with the NEWSPAPER SOCIETY on agency recognition.

NPD. New Product Development. Although most of the work in this field is carried out by specialists, ADVERTISING AGENCIES can be involved at many stages of the process; for instance, in working out the BRAND PERSONALITY and BRAND POSITIONING at an early stage, and in creating advertising, which has a key role to play in establishing the new BRAND in the market.

(Reprinted by kind permission of ADMAP)

NRS. National Readership Survey. The official survey managed by JICNARS, the Joint Industry Committee for National Readership Surveys on which the media, the advertisers and the agencies are represented.

NRS covers over 220 national publications. The sample is around 29,000. Results are published every six months and have been continuous since 1956. The survey gives readership figures and breaks these down into standard DEMOGRAPHICS (age, sex, region, social class, etc.). A number of other classifications (petrol-buyer, terminal education age, ownership of durables, holiday-takers, for instance) are included, as well as TV viewing, reading frequency and readership profiles. Other breakdowns, not published, can be obtained (e.g. by ACORN areas and Sagacity groupings – see GEODEMOGRAPHICS, LIFE STAGES) and computer access is available to MEDIA PLANNERS.

The QUESTIONNAIRE is designed to generate two main classes of information about readership: average issue readership and reading frequency. As described in the NRS survey (January–December 1986): 'The principle of measuring "readership" which has been used in these surveys since their inception is to attempt to establish at each interview whether or not the person interviewed has looked at any copy of the periodical in question during a period back from the day of interview equal to the interval at which the periodical appears. (Reading on the actual day of the interview is not included.) Thus, for each daily paper the survey attempts to establish whether or not the person interviewed looked at a copy of it "yesterday", the day before the interview. . . . For each Sunday paper or weekly magazine, the survey finds out whether or not the informant has looked at a copy of it in the past seven days, and for each monthly magazine, whether or not he has looked at a copy of it during the past four weeks.'

The questionnaire also aims to establish reading frequency of publications over the past year. There is also a series of questions about other media, the informant, his activities and his household. This enables detailed readership profiles to be built up which can be relevant over many different product fields.

NRS has been described as 'the bible of the space salesman and the media planner'* and the basic tool for anyone planning press advertising campaigns. In addition it is the largest continous random sample of the population generally available.

O

OFT. Office of Fair Trading, set up under the Fair Trading Act 1973.

Part of its function used to be to act as an advertising backstop – e.g. fostering codes of practice negotiated with the relevant Trade Associations, one clause of which is always a requirement that any advertising be bound by BCAP. With the implementation of the EC Misleading Advertising Directive, OFT will now have powers to take legal action to stop an advertisement as a back-up to self-regulation (see ASA). OFT has also initiated some legislation affecting advertising, e.g.

- Regulations under the Consumer Credit Act (1974) lay down, among other things, that all advertising on credit terms must express the interest in terms of the Annual Percentage Rate of Charge (APR), and specify the content of short, intermediate and full advertisements.
- The well-meant, but since found incomprehensible and therefore unworkable, Price Marking (Bargain Offers) Order in 1979.

Omnibus surveys. A research 'vehicle' run in the same way as a quantitative survey by market research companies but, instead of the QUESTIONNAIRE dealing with a single project, it deals with a number of projects each of which has its own sub-questionnaire.

The market research company organizes the fieldwork and data processing, and the same disciplines and constraints apply to the design of the questionnaire and the sample as for any other quantitative survey. Some omnibuses specialize in particular TARGET GROUPS, e.g. motorists, teenagers, bank account holders. A client buys into an omnibus with the most appropriate sample, conditions and timing.

Anyone can buy into an omnibus survey. It is a cost-effective way to ask a large sample a limited number of questions or research a rather specialist sample, who emerge as a small sub-sample in the omnibus, but who would otherwise be very expensive to locate.

See also QUANTITATIVE RESEARCH, QUESTIONNAIRE, SAMPLE.

Opticals. Wipes, DISSOLVES, fades, flip-overs, are all optical effects added to the film after it has been shot. These and any titling (SUPERS) are put onto the film by a specialist optical house.

OTS/OTH. Opportunity To See/Opportunity To Hear. The notional number of times the viewer/reader/listener within the TARGET GROUP would have been able to see or hear an ad on TV or radio.

For TV, it is those present in the room, with set on, tuned to the programme, at the time of the clock minute during which the commercial was transmitted (see BARB).

For radio, it means those listening within the clock quarter-hour during which the commercial was broadcast.

For posters, it means those who passed the site, regardless of speed (see POSTERS).

OTS/OTH from one medium are not comparable with OTS/OTH from another, as definitions differ.

Over a campaign OTS/OTH are usually expressed as an average, e.g. 75 per cent coverage with an average OTS of 4.

See also EFFECTIVE COVERAGE/REACH, FREQUENCY, IMPACT, TVR.

It stands for Opportunities To Sneer

(Reprinted by kind permission of ADMAP)

Outdoor advertising. Posters and any advertising designed to be seen outside the home, e.g. on buses, trains, taxis, parking meters, bus shelters, stations, sports events. Many of the most famous early advertising campaigns used outdoor media, e.g. Guinness, the London Underground.

See POSTERS, SHEETAGE.

Overlap. Applies to TV areas in which 15 per cent or more of homes can and do watch two or more ITV stations, each for at least 2 out of every 10 hours spent watching ITV. Until December 1984 TCA regional data double-counted these homes, but since January 1985 figures have been for NET HOMES.

P

Packaging. Vital contribution to a BRAND, as it is how the consumer sees it at the point of sale (see BLIND PRODUCT TEST). Additional effects occur when the product is used in its package in social situations, e.g. 'when somebody takes out a pack of cigarettes, he is showing his card. He's saying – that's the kind of club I belong to'.* The label on the wine put on the table for guests, the 'designer' label showing on our clothes – all make statements about us.

Packaging has not only to strengthen the brand itself and tie in with the BRAND PERSONALITY, it also has to protect the product. The package designer has to be up-to-date with a number of different technologies: of the product's physical properties; mass packaging possibilities, new materials, processes and machinery; printing processes. There are also legal requirements for what has to be on the package describing the product, in addition to its own branding. These are reasons why much of the work developing packaging is done by independent specialist design groups who are in touch with manufacturers of packaging materials and machinery.

Page traffic. Measurement used in READING AND NOTING research to number, usually as a percentage, respondents who remember having read or looked at a page in the publication being researched (though not necessarily having remembered anything about it).

Page traffic scores are used: (1) to show that certain positions in a publication get higher readership (and thus more is charged for FACING MATTER); (2) to show that certain sizes are more economic; (3) to assess the value of colour; (4) to assess the value of repeated insertions (see WEAR OUT).

See READERSHIP.

Panel research. See CONSUMER PANEL.

Pantry check. An interviewer checks the contents of a household's pantry, refrigerator and/or freezer. Sometimes this is for once-off *ad hoc* research (to supplement a questionnaire); sometimes it is repeated over a period of time (part of a home audit panel); and sometimes the check is combined with a diary of household purchases.

Pass-on readership. Estimate of the number of people, outside the immediate household of the purchaser, who read the publication – e.g. in dentists' waiting rooms, hairdressing salons, public libraries. This can add significantly to a publication's readership as opposed to its sales.

See CIRCULATION, PRIMARY READERSHIP.

Paste up. Or mechanical. A CAMERA-READY page or advertisement, with the artwork and all the typematter stuck down on art board accompanied by transparencies for the colour process work where relevant. The image of each page or ad is transferred photographically directly on to the printing plates.

See PHOTOSETTING.

Peak time. Peak times are the most expensive times to buy advertising time on TV or radio because that is when the audience 'peaks'. The times vary depending on the day of the week and the ITV contractor. For instance, the September 1987 issue of BRAD shows that LWT's peak rates were 18.00–22.30 on Fridays, 17.30–22.30 on Saturdays, 19.30–22.30 on Sundays, Thames TV's were 17.15–23.20, Tyne Tees' were 17.40–22.40 Monday to Saturday and 19.20–22.00 on Sunday. The ILR stations' prime times also vary but were mostly 07.00–09.00 on weekdays, later on weekends.

Penetration. (1) According to Rosser Reeves: the number of people who remember your advertising (see USP); (2) In marketing: the proportion of consumers in any target group who use a brand or a type of product over a particular time period; e.g. brand A has a market penetration of 25 per cent (see FREQUENCY OF PURCHASE); (3) In media: proportion of the population reached by a particular medium. More usual terms today are COVERAGE, EFFECTIVE COVERAGE/REACH.

Personalization. People's ability to personify an inanimate object – an important aspect of establishing a brand and creating advertising.

See BRAND PERSONALITY.

Photosetting. Or phototypesetting or filmsetting. The newer typesetting technology using computers, cameras and film instead of metal. Text is set directly on film or photographic paper, from which negatives, film positives, plates or whatever is required for the printing process are made. For advertising purposes, this has the advantage that a very wide choice of typefaces and sizes is available at no extra cost.

Pilot work. The testing of any marketing activity (product, pack, ad, research) on a small scale prior to launching the full programme. For example:

- Structured surveys are 'piloted' with a small sample to optimize the order of questions, efficiency of the layout, instructions to the interviewer, etc.
- Pilot marketing of a new product aims to check all production, distribution and communication on a small scale, and correct faults which appear, prior to launching nationally.

PMT. Photo Mechanical Transfer. A photographic print produced for the PASTE UP for PHOTOSETTING.

Point of sale. Literally, the place where the sale is made. For FMCG this means the supermarket check-out, the sweet counter, the retailer. For MAIL ORDER it is the home. For buyers of industrial equipment it could be the works, a special exhibition or the technical press (see TRADE, TECHNICAL AND PROFESSIONAL PRESS).

Positioning. See BRAND POSITIONING.

The 1982 prizewinning ® Araldite poster which literally gave the medium a new dimension – a world first! The car, a Ford Cortina, was actually stuck to a metal bracket which in turn was bolted to the hoarding. It is an effective and witty demonstration of the power of the adhesive which was continued the following year with a series of posters, the first with one Cortina stuck on, the second with two and the third with a torn hole in the hoarding and the headline, 'How did we pull it off?' With acknowledgements and thanks to Ciba-Geigy Plastics and FCO. ® CIBA-GEIGY registered trademark.

Posters. Posters are a cost-effective way to achieve nationwide coverage in full colour. There are about 180,000 roadside poster sites in the UK today.

A snag for advertisers used to be the lack of standardized research data, but this has now been rectified by OSCAR (Outdoor Site Classification and Audience Research) which measures 'site passage' – the number of people estimated to pass one location, regardless of speed. This is the best OTS measurement for posters to date. Sites, which are subject to planning controls, are owned and leased out by independent contractors, 40 of whom belong to the Outdoor Advertising Association. The contractors also arrange site inspections – to check the condition of posters, etc. – at regular intervals.

Poster sizes are standard (see SHEETAGE) up to the very large SUPERSITES which vary and also, sometimes, allow for special effects.

PPA. Periodical Publishers' Association. Membership ranges from publishing giants to small independents and is estimated to account for 80 per cent of revenue from periodical publishing. The PPA's advertising committee's work includes: recognition of agencies and advertisers booking space; supporting self-regulation and observance of BCAP. It has also initiated and underwritten the PPA Mail Order Protection Scheme (see DIRECT RESPONSE).

Pre-empt. TV contractors' gazumping technique for maximising rates for particular spots there is a seller's market for. Because time on ITV, by law, has to be sold at RATE CARD rates, these are not negotiable. So the rates for, say, 30–second PEAKTIME spots are listed with a number of different prices. Buyer *A* books a spot at whichever of these prices he considers worthwhile, but if buyer *B* subsequently decides the same spot is worth more, he can book it at a higher price. 'Bidding' or 'pre-empting' in this way can carry on right up to cancellation date. One agency reckons that their buyers 'buy' every spot five times before transmission. This can be avoided by buying specifically 'non-pre-emptable spots'.

Premium offers. When merchandise is offered at a reduced price, or free when the product is purchased. Usually obtained by sending off a COUPON from the pack or some other proof of purchase(s), such as two labels. The 'premium' can be goods – rail tickets, films, bulbs, etc. – or money, in the form of coins or lower price for the next purchase.

This is a flexible type of promotion since there is a wide choice of what the premium offered will be and the duration of the offer. It is not difficult to organize since there need be no interference in packaging or production lines, and few, if any, demands on the retailer. However, it is important that what is offered is consistent with the BRAND and its BRAND PERSONALITY (see PROMOTION).

Presentation. Any meeting at which somebody 'presents' work to somebody else. People in agencies make and sit through lots of presentations – to each other, to conferences, to the client at various stages of producing campaigns, from market research people, from TV and film production companies, from design companies, etc. The most important presentation on each ACCOUNT is the big meeting at which proposals for the next year are presented to the top CLIENT people, which will include the advertising strategies, the new campaign(s), TV and films, etc.

See NEW BUSINESS PITCH.

Presenter. The person who talks about (presents) the product in a commercial. The presenter can be just VOICE OVER, never appearing but often immediately recognizable, e.g. as for Mr Kipling cakes. Some are stereotyped figures, e.g. the cheerful un-named housewives who talk about their washing. Some are named but otherwise unknown individuals, e.g. the owners who talk about their cats and Whiskas. Some are known and recognized TV personalities. Very occasionally the presenter is the client, e.g. Bernard Matthews. The choice of presenter (when used) is an important piece of casting as his personality directly affects how viewers perceive the BRAND and the BRAND PERSONALITY.

Press media. Everything printed which takes advertising. Established publications are listed in BRAD. In June 1988 there were: 12 national daily newpapers and 9 national Sunday newspapers (see NATIONALS); 109 regional daily newspapers and over 1,000 weekly newspapers (see LOCALS); 1 free daily newspaper and over 1,000 local free distribution sheets (see FREE SHEETS); over 2,000 'consumer publications' (see MAGAZINES); over 3,500 business publications, which include the TRADE, TECHNICAL AND PROFESSIONAL PRESS. In addition there are many titles which do not make BRAD, let alone the NRS, at all.

The press is an important medium for advertisers:

● It is highly selective, especially in the consumer and business sections as the editorial in these publications reflects the special interests of the readers.

● Press advertisements can contain detail and information

The top 15 titles (1987) in terms of the value of their advertising

Title	Rank order 1987	1986	Display expenditure 1987 (£000)	Change on 1986 (%)
Daily Mail	1	(2)	92,543	+15
Daily Express	2	(3)	86,944	+10
Financial Times	3	(1)	85,865	+ 4
Daily Telegraph	4	(6)	73,140	+16
The *Sun*	5	(4)	69,306	− 7
Daily Mirror	6	(5)	67,486	− 5
Sunday Express		(7)	54,430	
Magazine	7			+ 9
You Magazine	8	(8)	52,326	+19
TV Times	9	(9)	46,628	+10
Sunday Times		(11)	46.065	
Magazine	10			+16
Sunday Magazine	11	(10)	44,181	+ 5
Radio Times	12	(14)	37,884	+ 6
Sunday Times	13	(12)	37,843	+ 1
Sunday Express	14	(13)	37,170	+ 2
The Times	15	(16)	32,265	+ 7

Source: MEAL's 'Top 150 Titles 1987', as published in *ADMAP*, February 1988.

needing the careful perusal which is not possible for ads appearing on TV, radio or posters.

In its turn it depends on advertising revenue to meet costs and make profits.

Press release. One of the classic PR ways of communicating with the media. The practice of sending a 'blanket' release to a long list of contacts in the media, even if it is well-written and takes up only one side of A4 paper accompanied by a good photograph, has been superseded, by the best PR people, with a more subtle and targeted approach. They target the media carefully – whose readers/viewers are the ultimate target group, how are their 'stories' presented, is your story likely to fit in with their publication or programme? They target the editors and journalists – who would be interested, can they be given an exclusive angle? They telephone, make arrangements, set up photographic opportunities, etc. The actual press release is now a relatively small element in a serious PR campaign to get consumers to read or hear about a particular product or service.

Pre-testing. Refers specifically to testing advertisements before their scheduled appearance. All pre-tests involve exposing advertisements to a sample of people and questioning them about their reactions. But there is a wide variety in methods of exposure, the state of finish of the advertisements, selection of the sample and types of questions asked.

There are two divergent schools of thought about what pre-testing can achieve:

1 The first is looking for research on the basis of which to make decisions directly about the relative effectiveness of different ads or to measure whether an ad is above or below a previously established 'norm'. The pre-test methods preferred are quantitative, usually on 'finished' advertisements, often exposed in a made-up TV programme or magazine, and effectiveness is tested by awareness, recall, persuasion measures, attitude change, pre- and post-gift choice. The underlying model of the advertising process in such research tends to be the CONVERSION MODEL. It is

popular in the US, since findings can be quantified, alternative campaigns tested and the winners picked out.

2   The second is looking for research results to provide insights as a basis for judgement and for the process of innovation. The underlying model tends to be that brands are bought by the target group because they satisfy both functional/practical/ economic needs and expressive/symbolic/emotional needs, which the advertising has to communicate. So GROUP DISCUS-SIONS or DEPTH INTERVIEWS are used to explore people's responses to the ad or commercial as a whole, as well as the words and images used, and how these relate to consumers' needs, attitudes and likeliness to buy. This type of pre-testing is often part of a CREATIVE DEVELOPMENT RESEARCH programme with the advantage that it provides feedback to creative people rather than yes/no verdicts. It is used more in the UK than the USA at present.

Primary readership. The first reader of a publication, usually the purchaser and/or his immediate household.

See PASS–ON READERSHIP.

Private label. The term is synonymous with Dealer Brands and Own Brands in the UK, Distributor Brands in the USA. Used for products sold exclusively in retailers' own shops under their own brand name, made to their specifications. These are usually close copies of leading brands or commodities, e.g. instant coffee, tinned fruit, cornflakes. Today they are not necessarily cheap and nasty copies, though a few manufacturers of leading brands still refuse to make private label brands to be sold in competition with their own. Today retailers are innovative – to the extent of creating new markets with their private labels, e.g. the way big supermarket chains are now marketing private label wines.

The big growth of private label over the past 20 years has had a direct effect on distribution and advertising of FMCG brands, which are in competition for space on supermarket shelves. Often only the no. 1 brand is stocked in addition to its private label competition – which is bad news for the rest. Prices of private label goods are keen and represent good value for customers because direct distribution systems are so efficient.

It's hardly surprising that supermarket chains (Sainsbury,

What is it that makes Sainsbury's Manzanilla such a dry sherry? Water, of course.

About 20 kilometres north-west of Jerez lies the small fishing village of Sanlucar de Barrameda. It is here, and only here, that the uniquely dry Manzanilla sherry is made.

Sanlucar's coastal position gives it a cooler, more humid climate than that of Jerez.

Ideal conditions, in fact, for the development of 'flor', a film of yeast that forms naturally on the surface of the sherry in the cask.

Not all sherries develop flor, but those that do are destined to become drier and lighter than those that don't. And none is drier or lighter than Manzanilla.

Served chilled, as it should be, it has a crisp freshness that makes it the perfect aperitif. Some aficionados even claim to detect a faint salty tang on the palate.

Once opened, the bottle should be kept in the refrigerator and the contents consumed within three weeks. (Not a difficult task.)

It should also be no more than six months old when you buy it.

Unlike most wines, sherry does not improve with age in the bottle.

At Sainsbury's, you can be sure the Manzanilla you buy will be in the peak of condition.

It is supplied to us by one of the most reputable bodegas in Sanlucar, and our price ensures that it doesn't sit on the shelf for very long.

Indeed, a bottle of Sainsbury's Manzanilla costs no more than a bottle of ordinary sherry. Which makes it one taste that's easy to acquire.

Good food costs less at Sainsbury's.

Sainsbury's Fromage Frais. It ought to be sinful, but it isn't.

For years the cream people have been talking about naughty but nice.

Now there's something you can use that's just as nice but not naughty at all.

Fromage Frais is a delicious low-fat soft cheese, with a light texture and a smooth, creamy taste.

Sainsbury's sell a 1% virtually fat-free variety that has only 45 calories in every 100 grammes. (Hardly more than the average apple.)

There's also an 8% variety (with fresh cream folded in) that contains less than half the fat of single cream.

All our Fromage Frais comes from a family-run dairy in France and is made as only the French can make it.

In France, no self-respecting cook would be without a tub of natural

Fromage Frais in the fridge. Each year they get through 400,000 tonnes of it.

They spoon it on to fruit. They spread it with jam on croissants. They dollop it on baked potatoes with chives and black pepper. They stir it into sauces.

In short, there's hardly a meal that Fromage Frais can't improve.

To give you some ideas we've produced a free recipe leaflet.

In it, you'll find simple dishes (like the baked potato) and recipes for the vegetable hot-pot and raspberry cheese whip you see opposite.

Why not pick up a leaflet with your Fromage Frais and add pleasure to your cooking without inches to your waistline.

Good food costs less at Sainsbury's.

Sainsbury has been one of the most successful retailers in developing their private label into a brand that combines freshness, quality and good value. These ads, originally in full colour, have great sensual appeal. The food and drink, which are a little out of the ordinary, look so inviting your immediate response is: 'That looks so good, I must try some.' Created by Abbott Mead Vickers•SMS Ltd on behalf of J. Sainsbury plc.

Tesco, etc.) have developed their private label so energetically. Increasingly, long-established pioneers in other product fields – like Marks & Spencer (St Michael) and John Lewis (Jonelle) – are being followed by other retailers, like Dixons and Currys.

See BRAND.

Product. The product is what the manufacturer produces – what comes off the production/assembly line.

Its transformation into a BRAND starts with its packaging, its pack design, its name, the price it's sold for, its advertising and promotions and PR. Some products manage to emerge as brands without any advertising; most have to try harder.

Product lifecycle. Theory that a product's life is in four stages: introduction, growth, maturity, decline. At its introduction the product meets new needs, and sales grow, but eventually a new product fills those needs better, and sales decline. The cycle varies depending on the product – some (Royal Wedding souvenirs) have a very short life, others (like hammers and nails) a long one. New technology cuts some lifecycles off in their prime (the advent of nylon net curtains killed lace ones).

A BRAND is not so vulnerable, because it can be adapted and brought up-to-date to meet new needs, use new technology. Many famous brands have kept alive well beyond their natural span in this way. Think of Oxo, a brand which existed pre–1914, reached peak sales in the hard times of two World Wars, then during the never-had-it-so-good late 1950s was re-packed, re-launched, re-advertised and, over the next 20 years, reached new peaks of sales and profits. Think of the way some brands of washing products have been rejuvenated since the 1930s – progressing from soap powders to detergents to biological action and now, in some cases, to concentrated liquids.

It can become a self-fulfilling prophecy if, when a brand's sales slip, it is decided that the decline stage has been reached and so sales and advertising support are cut back, with the result that sales slip even further.

Product testing. Measuring how people evaluate the physical properties of a product, especially if it is a totally new one or an improved existing brand. The aim is to discover if it performs, is

relevant, offers more than the competition, satisfies a need. Methods can vary. Tests can be organized in a home environment or a testing centre (hall or mobile van, see HALL TEST). The sample can be asked to assess one single product fairly comprehensively, or rank several in order of preference. The sample can also vary from a small one-off sample of a broad target group to a large permanent panel – as used by some big companies which are continuously engaged in product testing.
See BLIND PRODUCT TEST.

Production company. TV commercials and films are produced by independent production companies. Some are large with directors, editors and crews on contract, editing and processing facilities; others are tiny freelance outfits headed by one freelance director. Some specialize in particular techniques. The whole industry clusters round London's Soho.

Ideas and STORYBOARDS are usually worked up in agencies which then work with a production company. This is so that the finished film follows the CREATIVE BRIEF.

Costs are extremely high, although competitive tenders are always sought by agencies. £250,000 is nothing out of the ordinary to pay for a 30–second commercial. Distant locations, special animation technologies, Busby Berkely sized casts to sing and dance – all add noughts on to the quotes. So can wanting a director like Adrian Lyne after he's become famous for his feature films. Economizing on the crew is not possible as the ACTT, their trade union, dictates numbers and rates of pay.

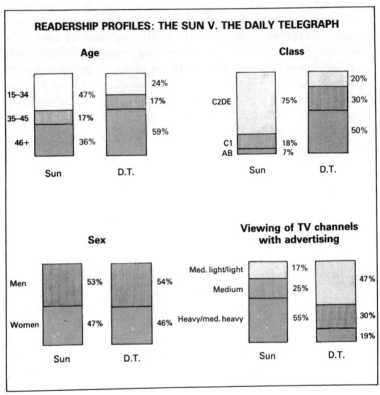

READERSHIP PROFILES: THE SUN V. THE DAILY TELEGRAPH

Age

	Sun	D.T.
15–34	47%	24%
35–45	17%	17%
46+	36%	59%

Class

	Sun	D.T.
C2DE	75%	20%
C1	18%	30%
AB	7%	50%

Sex

	Sun	D.T.
Men	53%	54%
Women	47%	46%

Viewing of TV channels with advertising

	Sun	D.T.
Med. light/light	17%	47%
Medium	25%	30%
Heavy/med. heavy	55%	19%

Source: JICNARS/NRS, 1987

Profile. As used in media research, a statistical summary of characteristics of a group of people – e.g. readers of a publication or viewers of a programme – taken from NRS or BARB. Used (sometimes rather creatively) by the media to sell their own particular space/time. Used by MEDIA PLANNERS to select the TARGET AUDIENCE most closely matching the TARGET GROUP – always a compromise as they are not presented in the same terms.

Progress department. Also known as Production, Traffic or Control department. The department in an AGENCY which makes things happen; the ACCOUNT EXECUTIVE'S non-commissioned officers. Their job is progress chasing and keeping the records of everything done on an ACCOUNT. They oversee every stage of production, check that dates are kept to, that ARTWORK arrives and that the finished press ads meet publications' deadlines in the right form and sizes. They do the same for all other press production jobs and for the agency's film, TV and radio productions.

Like the runner's job in a film production company, a job in the progress department has often been the first step to a seat on the Board.

Projective techniques. Range of unstructured interviewing techniques borrowed from psychologists to explore the private end of the public/private scale of ATTITUDES. Experienced interviewers work with small groups or individuals, sometimes on one occasion, sometimes several times over a period (see SENSITIVITY PANEL). The underlying attitudes, associations and ideas revealed are particularly stimulating to creative people.

Techniques include: role playing (let's pretend); fantasy situations (you are an object); sentence completion and word association; fantasy solutions/future scenarios (dreaming help-fully); psychodrawing/psychodoodle/psycholumps; cartoon/picture interpretation; story completion. Respondents' answers are not taken at face value, but interpreted by the interviewer within a pre-established psychological framework. This puts a high premium on the integrity and experience of the interviewer.

Promise. Dr Johnson's perceptive verdict on advertising: 'The soul of an advertisement is Promise, large promise.' Now, less elegantly, expressed as the KEY FACT or the single-minded PROPOSITION.

Promotion. Any activity which is intended to affect sales directly.
- Designed specifically for retailers, to encourage stocking up with and displaying the BRAND. Such 'incentives' can range from supplying one free unit for every 12 sold to elaborate competitions with Caribbean cruises as the prize.
- Aimed at the consumer, e.g. BELOW-THE-LINE activities such as COMPETITIONS, COUPONS, FREE OFFERS, PREMIUM OFFERS, money-off, SELF-LIQUIDATING OFFERS and any in-store MERCHANDISING.

Promotions have been described as offering temporary added value to a brand. However there is some evidence that even if a promotion increases sales and/or retailer stocking-up in the short term, brands which rely heavily on promotions rather than ABOVE-THE-LINE advertising tend to lose out and become less valued and eventually less profitable (e.g. the now often-quoted Andrex/Delsey history).★

Promotions also have to complement the normal positioning and personality of the brand, so that attitudes towards it do not change for the worse. This means that the nature of the promotion must be considered carefully.

Proposition. Defined by Reeves as 'one strong claim or one strong concept . . . that the competition cannot, or does not, offer' (see USP). Still at the heart of many advertising methodologies: as the first step on the way to finding the big ADVERTISING IDEA; as the basis for discriminating the BRAND from its competitors. For example, one agency puts in its statement of brief:

The single-minded proposition
Our advertising is characterised by one linking factor – it tries to make a single-minded proposition come alive in a compelling way . . .

Proposition is used today almost interchangeably with CONCEPT, and is therefore thought by some to be as testable; see CONCEPT TESTING.

Psychographics. Segmentation of people by their psychological make-up. It developed from 1950s MOTIVATION RESEARCH to bring human beings into the 'wasteland of percentages' that had dominated MARKET RESEARCH up to then. But quantifiable form was still important to allow for complex multivariate statistical analysis.

The only zero we recorded was while measuring recall of editorial content

(Reprinted by kind permission of ADMAP)

An early example, carried out by Wells and Tigert★ for Leo Burnett added 300 'activity, interest and opinion statements' to a questionnaire sent out to a Homemakers' Panel in the USA. Respondents had to indicate their degree of agreement with these on a six-point scale. Distinct, but unsurprising, different behaviour patterns emerged. Two of the most sharply differentiated groups were portrayed as 'The Swinging Eye Make-Up User' and 'The Heavy User of Shortening'. In a very broad way the personalities and the type of products used by the members of each group clustered (see CLUSTER ANALYSIS) very satisfactorily, but no evidence was supplied as to whether these tied in with brand choice. This research, linking psychographics with normal demographic information and product use, was seen as providing a useful insight into characteristics of a target group.

A lot of subsequent studies in the USA and the UK have identified psychological and personality traits and linked them with product and media use, some more successfully than others (see LIFESTYLES). For the mass of frequently-bought household products, no psychographic segmentation has really proved to be a more accurate discriminator of brand choice than the ordinary SOCIO-ECONOMIC CLASSIFICATION. It seems that choice of brands in these product fields is generally too trivial a matter to be much affected by fundamental differences in psychological make-up.

But for the infrequently purchased products which are more self-expressive 'style' items – such as cars, clothes, furnishings, holidays – the psychographic approach can be revealing and helpful (see BRAND LOYALTY).

Outlook,† a recent LIFESTYLE classification, has shown that in some sections (e.g. leisure – pub-going, package holidays, theatre-going, visiting museums) their groupings discriminate better than the standard social grades. Their financial sector showed, as one might expect, that social class still prevailed.

Another recent use of psychographics in a different way is made by SRI's Values Attitudes and Lifestyles (see VALS).

Public relations. 'The deliberate planned and sustained effort to establish and maintain mutual understanding between an organisation and its public' is the Institute of Public Relations' definition of PR. In other words, all a company's communications, internal and external, which are not advertising – e.g. paid for space or time in the media (see ADVERTISEMENT). But to be really effective, advertising and PR need to be closely co-ordinated, each working in its own way towards the same objectives (see CORPORATE ADVERTISING).

Cultivating the media is in any case only one aspect of PR. Every interface between company and public is important. A detail like Bernstein's★ airline which played 'Something's go to give' on take-off, or the design of the CORPORATE LOGO, are both links in a chain which can also include big money sponsorship of sport or an arts project, a stand at a major exhibition or how company pensioners are treated.

PR people are employed within companies at different levels under a confusing array of names. At the top a Director of Public Affairs might be on the board; departments can be called Public Information, Investor Relations, Corporate Communications, Employee Relations, Publicity, Consumer Services, Customer Relations or any combinations of these. Outside PR consultancies vary in size, specializations and fees. IPR (Institute of Public Relations) members (who are individuals, not companies) have a code of practice. Members of the PRCA (Public Relations Consultants Association) are organizations and respect a similar code.

See also PRESS RELEASE, SPONSORSHIP.

Q

Qualitative research. Research using a comparatively small sample with the objective of gaining insights, rather than generating numbers. Qualitative research is essentially exploratory, diagnostic and is used increasingly to build up background information – e.g. to identify behaviour patterns, beliefs, opinions, attitudes, motivations; to establish priorities; to generate hypotheses for further investigation; to test responses to products, ads, ideas; to discover more about private attitudes not revealed by direct questioning. It is especially valuable at the planning and creative stages of developing advertising (see CREATIVE DEVELOPMENT RESEARCH).

It is also used to provide a lead for questionnaires on larger-scale QUANTITATIVE and ATTITUDE RESEARCH, as well as to illuminate, interpret and fill out the necessarily rather superficial data provided by the latter.

Techniques are informal, semi-structured or unstructured (see GROUP DISCUSSIONS, DEPTH INTERVIEWS, SENSITIVITY PANELS, PROJECTIVE TECHNIQUES). Respondents are recruited to represent people from a given target group or section of the community.

The debate within the ranks of qualitative researchers is how far 'interpretation' should go. One view is that interviewers should not 'interpret' but stick to direct questioning and report back what their respondents say verbatim. This is the level on which much of the early MOTIVATION RESEARCH was done. The other is that the value of any qualitative research lies in identifying the underlying emotionally-based aspects of behaviour which are not easily expressed verbally (or truthfully) and only revealed through 'enabling' techniques carried out and interpreted by trained, skilled and experienced interviewers. This accounts for most of the more recent developments in techniques and practice.

Quantitative research. Research using a large enough sample of consumers to generate valid statistics so that market size, potential sales, target groups, etc., can be quantified. The size of the sample depends on the degree of accuracy required. Statistical theory enables us to predict the margin of error attached to any finding from a survey according to its sample size (see SAMPLE).

Sample size also dictates the use of structured questionnaires which are planned so that data can be analysed by computer. The validity of any survey is affected by the wording of the questions (see QUESTIONNAIRE) as well as the selection and size of the sample. The interviewer's job is simply to follow the questionnaire exactly.

Fieldwork is carried out either by face–to–face interview (in the home or the street) or by phone or by mail. For TV viewing figures an electronic device is used (see BARB). Big surveys are either one–offs, specially tailored for a particular client, like the newspaper opinion polls, or continuous, that is, repeated at intervals, such as NRS or the Family Expenditure Survey, which also enable trends to be identified. Some market research companies run surveys on to which anyone can have their questionnaires added, at a price (see OMNIBUS SURVEYS).

Questionnaire. The list of questions and instructions used in a structured interview.

The design of the questions is a skilled job on which success of the research depends; the classic text on this was written by Payne, in 1951.* For example, the way a question is worded will influence the response just as much as if it had been prefixed with *nonne, num,* or *ne.* It is well known that there are some questions which are never answered accurately – alcohol consumption, for example is invariably underestimated. There is also interviewer-bias because people (all over the world, not just in the UK) seem to have this pathetic instinct to please the interviewer with the 'right' answer.

In a well-designed questionnaire, the wording is clear, without ambiguity or bias. There are no unfamiliar words, difficult or abstract concepts to baffle the respondent. The interviewer may only ask questions as written. For 'closed questions' a selection of responses is given. 'Open-ended questions' mean the respondent answers in his own words. All are designed so that data can be analysed by computer – even the open-ended questions can have computer-aided post-coding. The order of the questions is important – to arouse interest, to get co-operation and to filter out those for whom the question is irrelevant. Prompt cards listing alternatives and/or attitude scales make less demands on respondents' memories. Questions about the respondent (age, sex, occupation, socio-economic class, etc.) are included to provide a check on both the SAMPLE and the profile descriptions of sub-groups. Nearly all questionnaires are piloted so that their wording and layout are optimized before the actual (and expensive) fieldwork starts.

The interviewer carrying out a structured questionnaire is not expected to contribute at the time of the interview apart from, sometimes, selecting the required sample. Researchers doing qualitative research have greater responsibilities, normally working from an Interview Guide and providing their own reports and interpretations.

Quota sample. See SAMPLE.

"What brand comes to mind when I say hoovers?"

R

R&D. Research and Development. The R&D department is where the manufacturer's team develops new products. Some departments are very high-powered, working at the frontiers of biochemistry; others are more down-to-earth, extending a range of confectionery.

Random sample. See SAMPLE.

Rate card. List of charges, plus any discounts or surcharges, made to advertisers by each publication, TV contractor, radio station or media owner. Press rate cards are regarded by MEDIA BUYERS as the basis for negotiation rather than statements of a fixed price. But as every TV spot must be sold at the rate published on the rate card, TV contractors' cards are long and complex, especially as they currently sell time for Channel 4 as well (see PRE-EMPT). Rate cards also show details such as page sizes, mechanical data (how the ad or commercial needs to be produced) and copy dates.

Rational appeal. Or the 'think' dimension in consumer response. It's about what a BRAND does, what it is for, what it contains, how it performs. *Which?* reports epitomize and sanctify the rational response. However its strength and importance vary with both the type of product and the individual who buys it. Several agencies (in particular Foote Cone & Belding) divide the thinking-oriented responses into high involvement (for purchases such as cars, consumer durables, financial offers) and low involvement (for news about habitual weekly household purchases). These are mirrored by similar variations in the feeling-orientated responses which treat EMOTIONAL APPEAL and SENSUAL APPEAL together. The ROLE FOR ADVERTISING for the particular brand infers what response is required, and how the different types of appeals are best balanced. (See also STIMULUS AND RESPONSE THEORY.)

Definitely a rational appeal – the phonecard is an eminently sensible idea, clearly demonstrated here! No emotional or sensual response necessary as there are no apparent taboos to overcome. With acknowledgements and thanks to British Telecom and the J. Walter Thompson Company Ltd.

Readership. Essential information for planning and evaluating any press campaign, but definitions vary. The most-used is that provided by the NRS. Starch and Gallup use different criteria (see PAGE TRAFFIC, READING AND NOTING) as do aided and unaided RECALL TESTS.

The discussion today is about how intensely an ad has to be read to be effective. Advertisers are not examiners – they just want to know whether readers are taking in enough to respond to the ad. Is 'eyes open in front of the page' or 'facing the page' sufficient? One view is that as the eyes scan the page, the right-hand side of the brain is noting what is there, but the interest and attention of the left-hand side is only triggered when an ad is sufficiently involving: the first type of perception can lead to recognition later, the second to recall. So, if 'ads are meant to . . . communicate as quick as a wink . . . 50% noting probably translates into something over 75% actual exposure.'* Another factor is the level of interest in the content of the ad: shoes tend to score well for women, cars for men; or its execution: this is what every DIRECT RESPONSE advertiser is measuring.

An attempt was made in the 1970s to measure readership by photographing eye movements (DEMOS – Direct Eye Movement Observations System). Apart from being very expensive, some people denied they had read what the camera had recorded them as reading.

Reading and noting. Tests pioneered in the 1930s by Starch (USA) and Gallup (UK) to show which editorial and advertisements in publications were read. Readers to be sampled were identified if they could remember one item in the issue to be 'starched' unaided. Then they would be taken through the whole issue page by page indicating which pictures, captions, headlines, copy they had seen/read, and each page was marked accordingly. A US study (*Printed Advertising Rating Methods*) has cast doubt on the reliability and meaning of reading and noting research: they found quite high 'recognition' scores for ads which had not actually appeared.

See NRS, READERSHIP.

Recall tests. In the conversion theory of the way advertising works, recall of the contents of the ad is an important and necessary step towards action (i.e. buying the product) so that recall tests are a valid measure of advertising effectiveness. They are also valid in the 'fame' theory – that advertising should above all be 'famous' and noticeable (see AWARENESS, CONVERSION MODELS, DAGMAR, ROLE FOR ADVERTISING).

In a recall test, respondents are asked if they remember an ad on TV the previous evening, in a daily paper on the previous day, in a magazine during the previous week/month. Recall is said to be proved if the respondent can reasonably accurately describe its contents. Unaided recall means that the respondent is

Recent advertising for VW is a recognizable descendant of the original Bernbach Beetle ads in that the appeal is rational and the presentation is stylish. The reader is made to think about the qualities of the Polo in this ad; the life-saving construction, for instance, as well as its design, colour and extras. This rational appeal persuades a certain type of person (the target group) to prefer the Polo to other hatchback competitors. With acknowledgements and thanks to Volkswagen (UK) Ltd and DDB Needham.

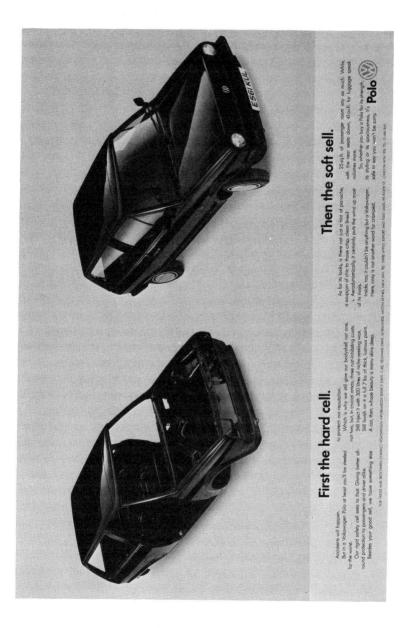

given no clues. Aided recall (more common) means that names of publications are shown to respondents: the NRS uses mastheads of daily papers to filter out readers from non-readers; the BBC used programme listings for checking TV viewing pre-BARB (see DAR). Sometimes (see READING AND NOTING), respondents go through the actual publication so that each part of the page or ad recalled can be indicated.

Recall tests are relied on more in the USA than in the UK today.

Reinforcement. Current thinking is that reinforcement is one of the most powerful ways advertising is effective, essentially by reinforcing existing consumer attitudes and habits rather than by converting them to new ones (see CONVERSION MODELS, ROLE FOR ADVERTISING).

Alan Hedges★ has pointed out that many everyday buying decisions are made at a very low level of consciousness. Reinforcement aims for responses like: 'That reminds me . . .', or 'I always knew I was right to . . . ', with the result that the BRAND advertised is always on the consumer's acceptable menu of brands (see REPERTOIRE).

Reinforcement is an equally important element in advertising for expensive infrequently-purchased consumer durables, such as cars or washing machines. Prospective buyers need to be aware of brands while they choose (even though something like two-thirds of car buyers apparently stick to the same make they had previously) and afterwards to reassure themselves they have made the right choice (see COGNITIVE DISSONANCE).

Repeat purchase. A repeat purchase is a second or subsequent purchase of a brand within a specified time (which can be as short as a week or as long as a period of years – see FREQUENCY OF PURCHASE). As commonly used, repeat purchase goods are products or services in which individual BRANDS are bought repeatedly by their buyers (see FMCG).

The repeat purchase rate of a brand is the extent to which people buy it repeatedly, and this can be expressed in several different ways. The information is collected from consumer panel data. Measuring the rate of repeat purchase of a particular brand is important:

- For media planning – so that scheduling can relate to the likely interval between purchases.
- For creative people – to know whether the target group can be assumed to be very familiar with the brand (frequently bought FMCG) or unfamiliar (infrequently bought CONSUMER DURABLES) (see ROLE FOR ADVERTISING).

Repertoire. A concept argued about during the 1950s and 1960s but take for granted today. Ehrenberg,* analysing consumer panel data, showed that the solus buyer of a brand (someone who buys no other) is relatively rare and relatively unimportant. Most people have their own short-list of brands they choose between – their repertoire of acceptable brands of fish fingers, toothpaste, air freshener and so on. This has important implications for the way advertising works. It makes CONVERSION theories mostly irrelevant. It supports the hypothesis that advertising's main effect, especially for FMCG, is one of REINFORCEMENT.

See BRAND LOYALTY, CONVERSION MODEL, DAGMAR, MARKET SEGMENTATION, SALIENCE.

Repetition. The number of exposures of an ad or commercial judged necessary for maximum cost-effectiveness. Below a certain number OTS/OTH, the response will be sub-threshold, i.e. not enough to repay costs. Above a certain number, diminishing returns apply, i.e. the additional response will be too low to be worth spending the money, if not positively counterproductive.
See FREQUENCY, RESPONSE FUNCTION.

Response function. Expresses in the form of a graph the notional increase in response for each extra OTS (or total responses for TVRS).
See REPETITION.

Response rate. The effectiveness of DIRECT RESPONSE advertisements and DIRECT MAIL shots can be measured by analysing the COUPON returns. When coupons are keyed, all aspects of the ads/mailing shots can be tested: the offer itself, the illustration, price, headline, copy, caption. The rate itself is generally expressed as number of replies received per thousand mailing shots, or for press ads, the number per thousand circulation or per pound spent.

Retail audit. Check on purchases, stocks, prices and sales in a representative panel of shops, as a continuous measure of what, in a market, is going into the shops, what is distributed and what is bought by consumers. Specialists such as Nielsen offer syndicated services on a variety of trades (e.g. grocery, food, drug, health and beauty aids, confectionery, home improvements and cash & carry) usually on a long-term contract giving monthly reports, but they will also carry out *ad hoc* checks. Such audits are important for efficient marketing management as they indicate the state of distribution of own and competitors' brands, and can indicate both long-term trends and short-term effects of advertising, special promotions, etc.

As the audit involves checking deliveries to shops, stocks displayed and in store, the whole process will be greatly simplified when electronic scanning (e.g. EPOS) is universal. Audits can also include reports on prices, position of brands, shelf-space given, promotions and special displays.

Retail Price Index. A measure of the rate at which prices increase for a 'representative' sample of goods and services bought directly by the public. Compiled by the Department of Employment every month. A representative selection of more than 600 goods and services in more than 200 towns are regularly priced, so approximately 130,000 separate price quotations are used each month to compile the Index.

Since 1956 the changes in spending habits of the average household, as revealed by the Family Expenditure Survey, have been used to keep the Index up to date.

Reversing out. Headlines or text printed in white on black or tone background. The metal forming the letters is removed (or reversed out) of the areas to be printed. It is almost invariably harder to read than the same thing printed traditionally – black on white!

Risk. Risk theory explains the selective attention given by consumers to advertising as the level of risk people perceive in the choice of one brand rather than another. It is used as one way of selecting the ROLE FOR ADVERTISING and the creative strategy. Risks are high, as are involvement and consumer attention, when you are choosing things where it matters a lot if the brand chosen does not perform as expected – cars, holidays, financial investments, medicines, expensive clothing are high-risk purchases. Risks, attention, involvement, etc, are low when your purchases are inexpensive and/or frequently bought: very little is lost if they don't perform.

Role for advertising. The way in which a campaign is intended to work, within a marketing plan. That depends on what is used as a model of how advertising in general works. Early models assumed that it works by CONVERSION. Later models were based on broader communication theories.

Dissatisfaction with the over-simplistic CONVERSION MODELS and BRAND IMAGE theory led to the recognition that advertising can work in many different ways. Deciding the right role for advertising for a brand in its particular circumstances has become one of the ACCOUNT PLANNER's most important tasks. More complex models, derived from the broader field of psychology, were developed. One of the first, in 1967, was Dr Timothy Joyce's model shown overleaf:*

In 1964 JWT developed their STIMULUS AND RESPONSE THEORY, and in 1975 a more detailed 'Scale of Direct/Indirect Responses to Advertising'.† A model like the one overleaf makes systematic EVALUATION possible.

More recent views have stressed the importance of the execution – the way an ad is filmed or presented – almost at the expense of its content. This view derives from the work of Bill Bernbach: 'If your advertising goes unnoticed, everything else is academic.' Taking this to extreme lengths, an advertisement is considered an 'event' in its own right. Advertising should aim to be 'famous', talked about. This is many 'creative' agencies' rationale. It assumes:

famous advertising = famous brands = successful brands

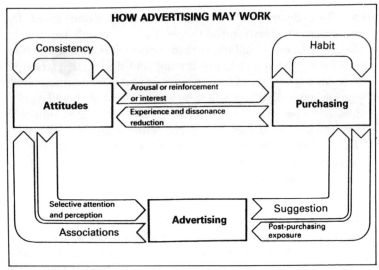

Source: Joyce, 1967

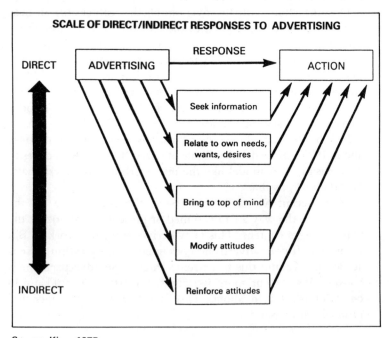

Source: King, 1975

Heineken and Benson & Hedges are quoted as examples of the success of this approach to advertising.

The style of its advertising is clearly part of a brand's personality. But 'advertisement as event' has to overcome the relatively low importance that advertising has for most people. As Alan Hedges has pointed out: 'Advertising is just part of the background scene . . . Advertisements form part of the continual whirling mass of sense impressions which bombard the eye . . . hundreds if not thousands of pieces of advertising each day . . . which are relegated to very low levels of consciousness for the most part.'‡ (see also ADVERTISING IDEA). At the same time, evidence shows that people have become sophisticated consumers of advertising, visually literate about what the imagery and symbolism is getting at, appreciative of entertainment value and cleverness for its own sake, sometimes even agreeing the ads on TV are better than the programmes. 'The real question is not what does advertising do *to* people, but what do people do *with* advertising'.★★ So developing greater insight into, and understanding of, people's responses to advertising is crucial.

Rough. First developments of a creative idea, as scribbled down by an ART DIRECTOR – can be on the back of the proverbial envelope. Slightly more finished, the rough is the basis on which first discussions within the agency take place. At the next, more finished stage, roughs might be discussed with the client, or used for CREATIVE DEVELOPMENT RESEARCH.

Rough cut. Film/TV term. The first (pre–DOUBLE HEAD) stage in assembling the live-action shots and cutting them to the required length.

RPC. Readers Per Copy. This means the average number and is an additional measure to the audited CIRCULATION of a publication. It varies widely; *Do-it-yourself* has 22 RPC, *Choice* has under 2, *Sporting Life* has over 4.6, the *Sun* has 2.8 (NRS, vol.2, 1986). See READERSHIP, PRIMARY READERSHIP, PASS–ON READERSHIP.

RPM. Resale Price Maintenance. Like the agency COMMISSION system, RPM was undermined by the 1964 restrictive trade practices legislation. Before then a manufacturer had a list price below which his brands could not be sold, and he could enforce this by suing the offending retailer. The effects of the abolition of RPM were hastened by the growth of the MULTIPLES and in their turn helped them grow. Today the multiples can exercise enormous power over manufacturers.

Run of the week. Space in a daily newspaper booked to run any day of a particular week. Usually cheaper than space booked for a particular day.

Rushes. The first (rush) prints of a day's filming. The director selects the sequences he wants from these, and the editor uses them to put together the ROUGH CUT.

(Reprinted by kind permission of ADMAP)

S

Salience. A brand or advertising campaign is said to have salience when it is so relevant to the consumers' needs and desires that it is at the forefront of their minds (see ROLE FOR ADVERTISING). Salience scores are used to evaluate brand *A*'s salience relative to the competition over a period of time; e.g. consumers are asked to name toothpastes as they come to mind – first brand mentioned scores 5, the second 4 and so on. Brand *A*'s score is aggregated and compared with competitors' scores. The brand with the highest score wins on salience.

Sample. A limited number of people selected from any complete group (or population) so as to be representative of it. By researching the sample we can get information about the whole relevant population within acceptable margins of error. The sample size needed for any survey involves balancing the cost with the accuracy required. The statistical theories of sampling can be used to work out the likely error involved in any particular sample size, but they are quite complex. We can get a rough guide from the handy formula:

$$SE = \sqrt{\frac{p \times q}{n}}$$

(where SE = standard error, p = the percentage with some attribute, q = the percentage not having the attribute, n = sample size).

So if 40 per cent have heard of our brand and 60 per cent have not, in a sample of 600 the standard error is:

$$\sqrt{\frac{40 \times 60}{600}}, \text{ or } 2$$

According to statistical theory, this means that the chances are 68 out of 100 that the true number of those who have heard of our brand lies between 38 and 42 per cent (one SE either side of the sample's percentage), 95 out of 100 that it's between 36 and 44 per cent (two SEs) and 99 out of 100 that it's between 35 and 45 per cent (two and half SEs).

If this is not accurate enough for us we would have to increase the sample size. But it could be expensive, as we'd have to quadruple it in order to halve the standard error.

Such calculations assume that the sample itself is free from bias (which might arise from incomplete lists, non-response or faulty weighting) and is a *random sample*. That is, the respondents are drawn by chance from a complete list, such as the electoral roll. But most commercial surveys use *quota sampling*, in which the interviewer is given a quota (e.g. 10 ABC1 women under 45, 10 C2DE women over 45, etc – see SOCIO-ECONOMIC CLASSIFICATION) and selects the respondents herself. This can introduce bias, so that while quota samples are cheaper, they are less reliably representative than random samples.

Sampling. Giving selected households or purchasers an opportunity to try a new product free. There are many ways of organizing this: special small packs delivered as a DOOR DROP; small packs banded onto another of the manufacturers's products stocked by retailers; shop demonstrations.

For sampling in its market research sense, see SAMPLE.

Schedule. The media plan. Showing publications, TV, radio, outdoor – all the media to be used in a campaign with details of dates, spaces/times and costs. Also contains a breakdown of COVERAGE, FREQUENCY, OTS/OTH and TVRS.

A first schedule is drawn up as part of the campaign planning process. Changes are made as the results of analyses are studied, and the availability of times/spaces and final budget decisions are made.

Screen. Print term. Illustrations and photographs to be reproduced by half-tone blocks are processed into dots through a grid or screen with varying degrees of fineness. The greater the number of lines to the inch/centimetre the finer the reproduction. Smooth surface paper can take a fine 133/54 raster screen, newsprint takes a coarse 55/22 raster screen.

See BLOCK.

Script. The copy for film, TV or radio commercial. Indicates, on the left, what the visual treatment (the VIDEO) will be –

sometimes this is quite detailed indicating close-ups, etc., at others more descriptive (can become a mini-novel) to set a mood or atmosphere. On the right, is the complete soundtrack (the AUDIO), which indicates words said and by whom, SFX, music, etc., in the appropriate place. Overleaf is an example of a prize-winning Heineken Radio Script.

Self-liquidating offer. A premium offered to the consumer in return for proof of purchase plus money. The term 'self-liquidating' applies to the costs to the manufacturer which are nil, as the money paid by the consumer is calculated to cover the wholesale price of the premium, any handling or postage costs and sometimes advertising costs too. The offer is self-financing. The advantage to the consumer is that goods bought this way still cost significantly less than they would in a shop.

Sensitivity panel. Takes the EXTENDED GROUP one stage further – 10 respondents are carefully selected, trained and convened for up to 8 or more 4-hour sessions over a period of several months.
The training aims to make members of the group more aware of their senses. They are given practice in putting sensations into words and in participating in PROJECTIVE TECHNIQUES generally.★ Simultaneously the members develop a high level of trust which removes defensiveness, embarrassment, self-consciousness – the barriers to free expression. This happens more quickly if they have been selected with an eye to compatibility (similar age, class, situation). Intelligence, creativity and a stable personality are other important criteria. Schlackman's† experience is that 'it is . . . the finest way to generate hypotheses for further market research.' Fuller has used sensitivity panels successfully for new product development and developing images about brands. Their big disadvantage is that they are very expensive to run.

Sensual appeal. The way a BRAND looks, feels, sounds, tastes, smells, makes up its sensual appeal and provokes our response to it on that level. The design of the product itself affects us, as does its packaging, even with functional products like washing machines and vacuum cleaners. Advertising, particularly with good art direction, can bring out elements that people might not

---

LOWE HOWARD-SPINK

ROWATER HOUSE 68-114 KNIGHTSBRIDGE LONDON SW1X 7LY TELEPHONE 01-584 5033 TELEX 25109

XXXXXNXKXXX RADIO

CLIENT:	**WHITBREAD**	TITLE:	**"THE CANBUSTERS"**
PRODUCT:	**HEINEKEN**	JOB NO:	
DATE:	**31 March 1988**	LENGTH:	**70 seconds**

(Final production script - re-done as original was incorrect from 9 May 1985)

VIDEO   AUDIO

(Drone of aero engines. Heavy flak and aerial bombardment.)

CAPTAIN: Report damage, Hoskins.

HOSKINS: Flaps gone, Sir.

CAPTAIN: Check.

HOSKINS: Undercarriage shot away, Sir.

CAPTAIN: Check.

HOSKINS: I can't quite see the port engines from here, Sir.

CAPTAIN: Why's that, Hoskins?

HOSKINS: The port wing's missing, Sir.

CAPTAIN: Dash! How's the radio?

HOSKINS: (Switches on - BBC voice with crackle: 'I'm fine, thank you'.)
            Radio's fine, Sir.

CAPTAIN: Any news from Tail End Charlie?

HOSKINS: Look he sent us a postcard yesterday, Sir.

CAPTAIN: Any parachutes?

HOSKINS: No, just the postcards, Sir.

CAPTAIN: Well, what about those twirly things that go round when
            you blow on them?

HOSKINS: What, parachutes, Sir?

CAPTAIN: No, like windmills.

HOSKINS: Dandelions?

CAPTAIN: No! Look, here's a clue - Mooooooo.

HOSKINS: Oh, you mean cows, Sir.

CAPTAIN: No, propellors.

HOSKINS: But you did a noise like a cow, Sir.

CAPTAIN: I can't do propellors.

HOSKINS: Oh well, let me try, Sir - Brrrrrrr.

CAPTAIN: Brilliant. Propellors.

HOSKINS: All gone, Sir.

CAPTAIN: What about the fuselage?

HOSKINS: Well, we lost that over Bremen, Sir.

.....Cont'd/

LOWE HOWARD-SPINK

HOWATER HOUSE 68 111 KNIGHTSBRIDGE LONDON SW1X 7LT TELEPHONE 01 584 5033 TELEX 25109

XXXXXXXXXXX RADIO

CLIENT: **WHITBREAD**	TITLE: **"THE CANBUSTERS"**
PRODUCT: **HEINEKEN**	JOB NO:
DATE: **31 March 1988** (Final production script)	LENGTH: **70 seconds**

VIDEO	AUDIO
2/	

CAPTAIN: Dash it, Hoskins, so there's nothing left of this plane?

HOSKINS: No, Sir. Sorry, Sir, but there's one last chance. If I could just reach ..... if I could just reach this ...

CAPTAIN: I'd do it myself, Hoskins, if it weren't for this dashed idleness...

HOSKINS: I've got it, Sir, a can of Heineken!

SFX: Sound of engines/propellors starting up.

(TO THE TUNE OF 'DAMBUSTERS'):

Hei-neken re-e-efreshes the parts

other bee-ee-eers cannot

re-ee-ee-ee-ee-ee-each...

(Repeat & fade)

A radio script for Heineken which shows how a really good advertising idea can be successfully developed for different media — the TV, the posters and this radio script all keep the same jovial fantasy going with refreshing ingenuity. With acknowledgements and thanks to Whitbread and Lowe Howard-Spink.

Spend all day in bed.
Go out in a duvet lined trenchcoat.

Khaki trench coat with red
trim and zip-in down
and feather lining
£99. Sizes 6–14.
Also available in
red with khaki
trim. 1st floor.

Red cord shirt £25,
matching cord skirt
with ruffle £29.
Sizes 8–16. Also in
beige and rust.
2nd floor.

Harvey Nichols, Knightsbridge, London SW1.

otherwise pay much attention to. The use of mouth-watering food pictures, designer room-sets, colour wherever possible in the press and on TV – all these focus on the sensual appeal of a brand.

PACKAGING has an important role too. For example, some foods are packaged to emphasize their RATIONAL APPEAL; with cool, rather severe labels they announce they are good quality, very hygenic and good value. Others major on the food itself in a much more obvious sensual way, showing perfect green vegetables or luscious ripe fruits, or prepared foods steaming and irresistibly ready-to-eat: see PRIVATE LABEL.

Even foods, though, do not rely on solely sensual aspects in their advertising. For example, Yorkie's chunkiness is about the sensual rewards of biting into thick chocolate, but its EMOTIONAL APPEAL is conveyed through the lorry drivers in its commercials who add another dimension of toughness and masculinity.

SFX. The way film people spell sound effects.

Share of voice. Adspeak for, usually, one brand's share of advertising expenditure as compared with its competitors in the same product field. Sometimes the term is imprecisely used to mean 'share of impressions', without taking size of space or length of spot into consideration.

Sheetage. Standard Poster sizes are expressed in sheets. Smaller sizes are double crown and quad crown. See below.

Show prints. The prints of films and commercials used for transmission in cinemas or for transferring on to videotape for TV. Also called *show copies, bulk* or *transmission prints.*

Stylish drawing and an amusing headline combine to make this coat extremely desirable. Most sensual appeals need the addition of colour, hence the beautiful colour photography which fills the fashion glossies. This is an excellent example of the black and white route fashion advertising takes when it appears in newspapers. With acknowledgments and thanks to Harvey Nichols.

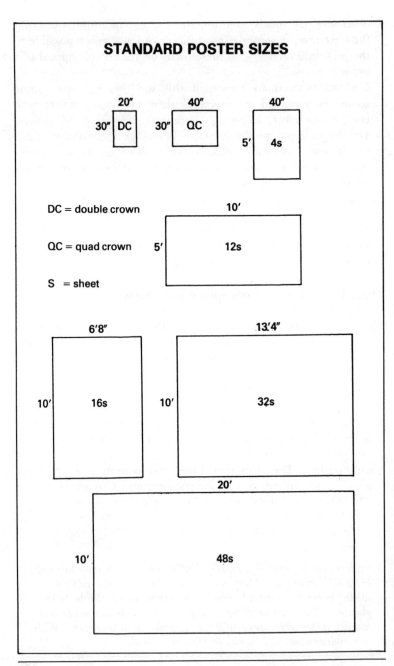

Showreel. Everyone connected with film or TV advertising puts together their own showreel – the best examples of their own work. Indispensable marketing device for AGENCIES to impress potential new clients, for writers and directors to get new jobs, for the production companies to keep working.

Silkscreen. Simple form of printing used mostly for packaging and point of sale, and by artists who like the medium. The image is transferred through a fine mesh screen, with a separate stencil for each colour to block out whichever part of the design is not to be printed.

Slice of life. Style of realistic TV production. The camera as fly on the wall happens to catch the real-life moment when a BRAND is being used and appreciated naturally – Maureen Lipman on the phone for British Telecom is a beautiful slice of life. Unfortunately the style is frequently debased, e.g. to kitchen scenes where one housewife is unnaturally knowledgeable and enthusiastic to another about how she cleans the floor.

Slogan. What advertising used to be about. A 1913 Manual, the *Advertiser's Pocketbook*, says: 'The object of a slogan is to assist in selling goods by fixing itself in the reader's mind so that he will always associate it with a particular article, service, place, etc. A slogan should be short and pithy, except when it is a rhyme, in which case it is necessarily longer . . . .' Two early examples are quoted: 'Good morning! Have you used Pears' Soap?' and 'Underground to anywhere, quickest way, cheapest fare.'

The best slogans are more memorable than those. Pre-war the slogan was often the heart of a poster campaign: 'Prevents that sinking feeling' (Bovril), 'Keep that schoolgirl complexion' (Palmolive soap), 'Guinness is Good for you' and 'Guinness for strength'. More recently Heineken and Heinz have created winners.

Although a memorable slogan obviously contributes to REINFORCEMENT, as the psychology of buying, choosing and communicating is explored in greater depth, the old emphasis on the slogan or catch-phrase has faded. Two Esso campaigns illustrate this: one in the 1960s majored on a cartoon tiger with

*One of the most memorable slogans coined in the last thirty years –
for Heinz Baked Beans. It has enlivened many a poster campaign.
But is has also been used very successfully to integrate TV, press and
poster campaigns. On TV, for example, it reinforces a more
complex story: this illustration is the way some recent commercials
ended. With acknowledgements and thanks to H. J. Heinz Company Ltd. and Young & Rubicam.*

the slogan 'Put a Tiger in your Tank'; the other is exemplified by
their subsequent use of a real tiger, brilliantly photographed and
filmed, as the personification of the brand and METAPHOR for it.

Socio–economic classification. One of the standard DEMO-GRAPHICS used to divided up the population for research and analysis – the nearest we get to the slippery concept of social class. As developed for NRS and widely used for advertising

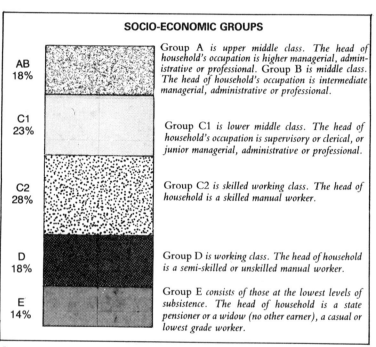

SOCIO-ECONOMIC GROUPS

AB
18%

Group A *is upper middle class. The head of household's occupation is higher managerial, administrative or professional.* Group B *is middle class. The head of household's occupation is intermediate managerial, administrative or professional.*

C1
23%

Group C1 *is lower middle class. The head of household's occupation is supervisory or clerical, or junior managerial, administrative or professional.*

C2
28%

Group C2 *is skilled working class. The head of household is a skilled manual worker.*

D
18%

Group D *is working class. The head of household is a semi-skilled or unskilled manual worker.*

E
14%

Group E *consists of those at the lowest levels of subsistence. The head of household is a state pensioner or a widow (no other earner), a casual or lowest grade worker.*

Source: JICNARS/NRS 1987

purposes, it is based on occupation of head of household, or chief wage earner and level of job responsibility.

Solus sites. Poster sites which stand alone, usually for 48-sheet posters (see also SHEETAGE).

Sponsorship. Form of PR which involves the provision of financial or material support by a company for some independent activity (often related to sport or the arts) not directly linked to the company's normal business. The sponsor hopes to benefit, usually from favourable attitudes to the company which develop as a result. It is not the same as patronage, which is given without expectation of a return in the form of publicity.

The main objectives of sponsorship are:

- To increase awareness of the company name or one of its BRANDS.
- To provide an opportunity to increase goodwill with trade customers.
- To enhance the company image in the community and boost employee morale.

Sponsorship can cost as much or little as you like and can therefore be very much less expensive than paid up advertising, although its effectiveness is even more difficult to judge. For cigarette manufacturers, denied TV advertising and strictly controlled in what can be said in the press or in the cinema (see CIGARETTE ADVERTISING) sponsorship is one of the few ways left to them to put their name before the public.

The companies/brands sponsoring sporting events may become associated with one covered by TV which offers mass exposure, e.g. the Cornhill Test, the Milk Cup, the Mars Marathon.

Sponsorship of the arts does not get quite that degree of exposure – often only a mention on the programme/catalogue or posters – unless it includes a charity performance attended by Royalty. These days scarcely a single opera, series of concerts or big exhibition is put on without some company sponsoring it. Current government policy is forcing the arts at all levels to look for sponsorship finance rather than central or local government funding. Information can be obtained from ABSA (Association for Business Sponsorship of the Arts).

Many local causes and events great and small also look for sponsorship. This can involve help in kind rather than money. It often produces positive results on the company's home ground, affecting employees, local consumers (or future ones) and the local authority favourably.

When deciding what to sponsor, the 'event' or cause is more likely to make a positive contribution to the company if it makes sense within the context of the company's activities, corporate policy or BRAND PERSONALITY. For example, the stamina needed to run a marathon exactly underlines what a Mars Bar is for; Olivetti's leadership in design was underlined by their sponsorship of the Venice Exhibition at the Royal Academy; the estate agent who gave out free Coca Cola at a street party is likely to be remembered when the residents come to sell their houses.

Stimulus and response theory. Communication theory which leads to the abandonment of the various CONVERSION MODELS. It is simply that communication is a two-way process. People are never passive recipients of communications of any sort, let alone advertisements – they respond actively and selectively. They bring their own ideas, they relate what they already know, or think they know, to everything they read or are told; sometimes in direct contradiction to it. They draw their own conclusions.

So advertising must also be a two-way process, and advertisements must be designed to stimulate, if possible, a specific response (see ROLE FOR ADVERTISING).

Sometimes the stimulus is more effective if it asks the reader/viewer to work a little. As Koestler said 'The artist rules his subjects by turning them into accomplices.'* People respond to stimuli on different levels (see EMOTIONAL APPEAL, RATIONAL APPEAL, SENSUAL APPEAL). When the desired response is analysed in terms like these, it gives a valuable guideline for setting advertising objectives, the creative brief and evaluative research.

Stop frame. Technique for animating inanimate objects – e.g. to create the impression that a pack has opened of its own accord. See ANIMATION.

Have you noticed how some people never like to say the word   ?

It's true   is a terrible disease, but it's not nearly as hopeless as it sounds.

In the past ten years enormous progress has been made in the treatment of

It is still, after road accidents, the major cause of death in children. But consider this.

Successful treatment of childhood   has risen from less than 10% in the 1950's to more than 50% today.

Many doctors are now convinced   will be the first cancer we will find a cure for.

With your help it will be.

Please give as much as you are able. Then by the year 2000, hopefully, people will no longer be scared to say the word

Because   will have disappeared forever.

PLEASE SEND DONATIONS TO THE LEUKAEMIA RESEARCH FUND, DEPT. SX, 43 GREAT ORMOND STREET, LONDON WC1.

Storyboard. The creative layout for film or TV commercial. A visual is developed in a series of sketches to show what will appear on the screen – indicating type of location, actors, treatment, how the product will be shown, SUPERS, etc. The sound track is typed in under the appropriate sketches.

Storyboards can be very roughly drawn or photographic. The final storyboard is used by the client, the agency and the production company as the reference point for the shooting.

Subliminal advertising. Banned by the IBA CODE and by the IPA for all its members since 1957. The idea that a name or picture may be flashed on a TV or cinema screen so fast that the audience does not consciously see it – but unconsciously responds – was popularized in the 1950s by Vance Packard in his alarmist book *The Hidden Persuaders*. But it now seems that the ice-cream experiment he used as his example never took place and nobody has managed to verify it since. An experimental single-frame 'keep watching' test broadcast was spotted by a test engineer, so it is unlikely any attempt to go subliminal would be unnoticed. VCRs, played back slowly, would also pick it up.

Supers. Lettering, prices, key phrases superimposed over film or video.

Supersites. Biggest poster sites, often taking 96–sheet posters and usually situated to dominate main roads with heavy traffic flows.

Superstores. Store with between 25,000 and 50,000 square feet of floor space. Numbers are increasing: in 1979 there were 211, by 1986 there were 432 and the pace is quickening as fast as planning permissions are obtained. Both superstores and the larger HYPERMARKETS are geared to customers shopping by car.

An appeal for donations which involves readers by demanding an effort from them; they must puzzle out who needs their help. It's an altogether different approach to advertising for a charity from the emotional appeal of the NSPCC advertisement (see p. 54). But no less effective. With acknowledgements and thanks to Saatchi & Saatchi Advertising.

Switch selling. Advertising one thing and then, when the customer tries to buy it, virtually forcing the purchase of something more expensive. It is banned in all advertising by both BCAP and the IBA CODE. BCAP's ban, under the heading 'Truthful Presentation: availability of advertised products', includes the advertiser's salesmen disparaging or belittling what has been advertised, recommending the purchase of a more expensive article, indicating unreasonable delays in delivery, or even just putting difficulties in the way of its purchase. An example is advertising ex-rental TV sets for £10, then selling customers a more expensive set because there were 'no more left' or 'believe me, Lady, it wouldn't last 10 minutes.'

Swot analysis. Strengths and Weaknesses, Opportunities and Threats. Headings under which the client's marketing plan for a brand are sometimes initially checked. Strengths could be excellent sales force and distribution. The weakness could be a product that was too ME-TOO (see INNOVATION). Opportunities could be identification of a new type of outlet – e.g. magazines in supermarkets. Threats could be heavy advertising expenditure by main competitors.

U.S.P today, alas, stands for Universal Supermarket Patronage

(Reprinted by kind permission of ADMAP)

T

Tabloid. Newspaper size favoured by popular dailies – approximately 300 mm × 400 mm. Half the size of BROADSHEET, which is approximately 600 mm × 400 mm.

Target audience. Target audience is the best match the MEDIA PLANNER or MEDIA BUYER can make to the TARGET GROUP specified for the CREATIVE BRIEF.

Target group. The consumers that the advertiser particularly wants to reach through advertising. In any market some people are more valuable than others – normally around a quarter of a brand's buyers account for around three quarters of its sales. Advertising cannot be aimed exclusively at that target group, because people's use of media does not tie up directly with their use of brands. But setting the target group can help to concentrate the aim, by a creative content that will particularly appeal to the target group, and by the right media selection (see TARGET AUDIENCE).

Definitions usually follow logically from the decision on the ROLE FOR ADVERTISING, and are set in terms of users, usage, attitudes and motivations. The most important and valuable target group is the one set in relation to usage in the market. DEMOGRAPHICS and LIFESTYLE help define users and match up market characteristics with media usage or personality characteristics. See also CREATIVE BRIEF, TGI.

Definitions will differ depending on what the target group is for. For example, when launching Krona margarine★ the creative target group was defined as 'housewives currently spreading salted butter, who are being forced to trade down because of the increasing price of butter, but who do not wish to sacrifice the taste and texture of butter.' The media target group was defined separately: 'the target consumers were seen primarily as housewives trading down from butter. . . . This definition was not of value in media selection. In fact the profile of margarine and butter users closely matches the population as a whole and demographics were expected to be less significant in selecting Krona users than attitude of mind. For the launch period the target group was therefore defined for media purposes as All Housewives.'

TC. Till Countermanded. Poster sites booked on a long-term basis by one advertiser until he decides to cancel. These were favoured in the past when advertisers like Guinness snapped up and kept their sites for decades, or agencies chose them to catch the client's Chairman's eye on his way to work.

TCA. Television Consumer Audit. An AGB household panel which surveys households' grocery purchases. 6,500 homes are audited and there are 4–weekly reports for each product field and brand covered in each TV area.

Telecine. TV system for showing films for viewing on a TV monitor or recording film on video.

Telephone research. Instead of being accosted on the street or at the door by an interviewer, the respondent is telephoned. Pioneered in the USA, and now feasible in the UK as telephone ownership has risen to over 80 per cent of households, telephone research has advantages of speed, control and cost–effectiveness. With CATI (Computer Assisted Telephone Interviewing) the data can be collected and analysed almost as the interview is taking place, usually within 24 hours.

The still–existing bias in telephone ownership, which is not a representative sample of the population as a whole, makes it difficult to design a sample for every target group. Methods of sampling are based on ways of generating numbers from the telephone directory or by random digit dialling or mixture of the two. Clients' lists can be used. Follow-up interviews are also possible from current or previous surveys. The questionnaires have to be specially constructed, above all to keep the respondent's interest alive. But with ingenuity even batteries of scales and prompted awareness lists can be handled. It is the ideal way to pre-test radio commercials.

Teletext. The common term for broadcast VIDEOTEXT. ITV's Oracle and BBC's Ceefax are both teletext services containing several hundred pages of continuously broadcast information, utilizing the spare lines of the standard TV channels. Oracle takes advertising, but the possibilities are still very restricted and mostly confined to pages of basic information.

Test market. Launching a new product with advertising, point of sale, etc., in one area or town to test the product itself and the elements of the marketing mix, and then using the results to project sales on a national scale. The essence of test marketing is the projection – to find out from a small scale experiment what to expect on a national scale – whereas PILOT WORK aims mainly to correct, modify, get bugs out of the system. So, although adjustments can be made to any of the elements before going national, each adjustment will make it harder to project accurately. It is therefore important when embarking on test marketing to be very clear what the object of the exercise is.

Testimonials/Endorsements. Strictly regulated in BCAP under the umbrella of 'Truth' (see also TRUTHFUL). For instance, if any advertiser wants to use a testimonial, consent must be obtained in the form of a signed and dated statement with the actual words used available on request. Moreover what is said must be true and in accordance with BCAP. If the glowing letter breaks other rules of BCAP, it can't be used. All claims have to be substantiated in the usual way.

There are specific regulations for slimming testimonials and no testimonials at all are allowed for CIGARETTES.

The IBA CODE is similar and also contains additional restrictions:

- On children's testimony – they can only make spontaneous comments, not give formalized personal testimony.
- On testimonials for medicines or treatments – no celebrities in public life, sport or entertainment, etc. can give one.

Royalty is out of bounds. Use of the Royal Coat of Arms and Cypher in an advertisement (and the symbol of the Queen's Award to Industry) is strictly controlled by the Lord Chamberlain's Office.

In spite of all regulations, testimonials are the basis of many famous campaigns. Early advertisers were unscrupulous in using testimonials, with or without consent. Not until 1928 was there a successful libel action against this practice: Tolley, a famous golfer, sued Fry's on the grounds that his amateur status was compromised by a testimonial ad which he had not consented to. He won £1,000 damages and established the legal precedent that *no* testimonial could be used without consent.

TGI. Target Group Index – a continuous survey run by the British Market Research Bureau. It consists of single-source data which combine brand and product usage data with media usage data collected from the same (huge – 24,000) sample of people. It helps to identify, describe and reach target groups by giving direct information on which publications are read by, say, occasional buyers of Heinz baked beans, so you do not have to rely on using broad and imprecise matching characteristics such as social class or age. It also reveals trends; the 1987/88 survey is the twentieth.

Tracking study. Repeated surveys using the same QUESTIONNAIRE to monitor something over a period of time. Examples are brand awareness, advertising awareness, attitudes to brands, brand preference, brand usage, etc.

Trade advertising. Manufacturers communicate with their retailers or distributors via the trade press (see TRADE, TECHNICAL AND PROFESSIONAL PRESS) or, very occasionally, on TV. As the main response required is for them to stock up, the advertisements are mostly about promotions, money-off, advertising plans, new lines – anything which could be said to produce more profits. Financial motivations are paramount, and, as in the financial pages of the press, terrible puns are the order of the day.

The British pre-war ideal of glamour – a combination of youth, beauty and aristocracy. Duchesses, Honourables and even Princesses all agreed to provide testimonials for Ponds beauty products (mostly Vanishing Cream and Cold Cream). This was the way Ponds positioned their products as both glamorous and proper for all the non-socialite, non-aristocratic women who, in those days, still aimed to be ladylike. The same campaign ran from 1935 to 1950. With acknowledgements and thanks to Chesebrough-Pond's Ltd.

THE LADY HELENA FITZWILLIAM

6 DAYS A WEEK IN THE SADDLE
but a *skin* any film star would envy

STUNG BY THE RAIN, spattered with mud, whipped by the wind, following the pack across plough and fallow and five-barred gate — hunting, *six days a week!*

Hunting is the breath of life to Lady Helena FitzWilliam — though she is anything but a hunting woman to look at. Far from being rough and "weather beaten," hers is the loveliest complexion imaginable — fair and fine and smooth of texture, and as fresh in colour as a wild rose.

" I know they say hunting's hard on the complexion," said Lady Helena, " and I certainly come up against some terrible weather. But I find I can keep my skin looking as I like it with the very simplest beauty-care. I use Pond's Creams."

You too can have a skin as lovely as Lady Helena's if you read these simple facts about skin beauty and follow her example.

Below the skin you see is your under-skin. A lovely complexion depends on the healthy condition of this under-skin. Before you reach your twenties the under-skin tends to grow sluggish. Circulation slows up. Tissues shrink. Glands get lazy. Soon enlarged pores and blackheads appear.

Here's the way to end these troubles. Cleanse your skin night and morning with Pond's Cold Cream. Its fine oils rouse the under-skin to vigorous action. Once more the blood flows briskly. Then tissues are braced — glands work freely. Blackheads and blemishes disappear. Again your skin looks young and fresh and lovely.

During the day, and after your nightly cleansing with Pond's Cold Cream, smooth Pond's Vanishing Cream on your face. Besides being a grand powder base, this cream feeds two beauty substances into your skin. One substance nourishes skin cells, guards against lines : the other, which is found in young, lovely skin, makes your face soft as velvet. Try Pond's Creams yourself, today. Jars or tubes *from 6d. each.*

HAVE YOU TRIED POND'S POWDER?

Write your name and address below, attach a 1d. stamp and post in a sealed envelope to Dept. P 0000, *Pond's, Perivale, Greenford, Middlesex, and we will send you FREE SAMPLES of all five shades of Pond's Face Powder — Natural, Peach, Dark Brunette, Rachel 1 and Rachel 2.*

NAME

ADDRESS

Trade, technical and professional press. All lumped together in BRAD as 'Business Publications', which may or may not be on general sale and are often sent to members of a learned, professional or trade association only. What is known as the 'Trade Press' by advertisers are those publications which provide a communication channel between producers/manufacturers and distributors/retailers. Producers/manufacturers use the trade press as a vehicle for announcing plans for advertising, special offers and promotions, new products, so stocks can be built up for when the campaign breaks.

Publications are self-identifying: *The Grocer, The Chemist and Druggist, Men's Wear, Hotel & Catering Review, Cash & Carry Wholesaler.* The adman's source is CAMPAIGN.

Occasionally TV is used, but so far only by really big spenders, such as the ITV companies themselves, and in addition to the trade press.

The technical publications overlap to some extent with the trade press, but also are sources of specialist information and, as such, used for business-to-business advertising to the relevant TARGET GROUP, although many have uncertified circulations. Titles include: *Middle East Electricity, Cargo Systems International, Process Engineering.*

Professional publications are those directed to members of the relevant profesion – medical, legal, architectural, educational, etc. Again valuable for reaching very specialized target groups. Some very learned journals do not take advertising, but all the titles in BRAD do.

Transmission. The actual time a commercial is on the air, i.e. being transmitted.

Punch, *like Ponds, positions itself by the people who are selected to provide the testimonials – here David Puttnam – then by the style of the writing with its idiosyncratic personal detail. Its success depends on people having a positive response to the testimonial. So, if you admire or like the people chosen, and are a regular reader, your choice of* Punch *is reinforced. If you are an irregular one you are reminded about it. If you have not seen it recently, you might be stimulated to try it out. With acknowledgements and thanks to* Punch *and Leagas Delaney.*

Transmission script. Final film or TV script with full details, including all SFX and music; artistes' names, when relevant are specified. This is a record of what has been filmed and the people involved.

See IBA and ITVA for stages of script approvals.

Transparency. Colour film with a positive image, just like your own slides. Can be viewed directly on a light box, or projected on a big screen, or used without further processing as ARTWORK.

Truthful. Fourth basic BCAP word (see also LEGAL, DECENT, HONEST). It is carefully defined in the sense of 'truthful presentation'. Its purpose is to prevent consumers being misled 'about any matter likely to influence their attitude to the advertised product'.

It details treatment of facts and opinions, testimonials, how to quote prices, the use of the word 'free', the identification of both advertisers and advertisements, etc. It also bans SWITCH SELLING – advertisers have to ensure that any product advertised is readily available.

Significantly, the only advertisements truthfulness need not extend to are political ones, unless appealing for funds. BCAP says 'to the extent that any advertisement expresses the advertiser's position on a matter of political controversy, neither the opinions thus expressed, nor any evidence which may be adduced in support or explanation of them are subject to the provisions of this Code'.

The IBA CODE simply says that all advertising must comply with the Trade Descriptions Acts and therefore not contain any 'descriptions, claims or illustrations' which could mislead viewers, directly or by implication.

As yet, advertising in the UK need not go to the lengths it has to in the USA, where only the real thing can be filmed or photographed, no matter what the problems. Here it is enough if the final picture does not mislead.

See ASA, COMPARATIVE ADVERTISING, TESTIMONIALS.

TV/film director. The choice of director, as much as the production company, if he works for one, affects the quality of the commercial. Many famous directors in the USA and the UK have made commercials and there are obviously would-be Hugh Hudsons and Alan Parkers somewhere. It is the agency's own TV PRODUCER's business to know who and where they are.

TV producer. The ADVERTISING AGENCY's link with the film PRODUCTION COMPANIES. If employed by the agency, the TV producer is part of the CREATIVE DEPARTMENT, where he may be head of an empire or a one-man band, depending on the outfit. There are also freelance producers.

The TV producer's primary responsibility is to work with the TV/FILM DIRECTOR and the production company to make sure that the finished commercial: (1) achieves the creative result envisaged by the agency's creative people and agreed with the client; (2) does justice to the vital ingredients of the film from the client/advertiser's point of view – e.g. treatment of his products and the way the commercial presents them. The TV producer's work is similar to a feature film producer's – the wheeling and dealing is only limited by the fact that he does not need to find the money, or stitch up distribution deals. So the responsibilities include:

● Seeing the production money is properly spent, that enough money is available to do the job properly, that the best quote is obtained and kept to, that the right essentials are paid and accounted for. The norm is 50 per cent up front to the production company and the rest paid in agreed stages.
● Organizing the day-to-day film-making: casting, finding locations, buying in music rights, progress chasing, ITVA approvals, repeat fees, etc.
● Knowing the work of directors and production companies in order to hire the best available for each particular job. This means getting in the SHOWREELS, keeping up-to-date with who is doing what, who is available, who is doing special deals, who is the up and coming Adrian Lyne, etc.

Like anything to do with the film business, getting into it is more than half the battle. You are on your own. There is no well-trodden path.

TVRs. Television Ratings. Units used to measure the TV audience, expressed as a percentage of the universe of viewers you wish to reach – as large or as small a universe as you like. An adult TVR of 20 on ITV means that 20 per cent of all adults receiving ITV were present in a room in which a TV set was switched on and tuned to ITV (see BARB for how viewing is now metered). Similarly 15 housewife TVRs means 15 per cent of housewives had the set on. A SCHEDULE of 6 spots each with 15 housewife TVRs aims for a total of 90 TVRs.

Type. All letters and characters, whether cast in metal or formed on a PHOTOSETTING or filmsetting system, are known as type.

Typeface. The style of the lettering. There are around 6,000 typefaces in existence, but only a fraction of these are in general use. The art of the typographer lies in choosing the typefaces most suitable for each job and specifying sizes and spacing. British Standard 2961:1967 classifies typefaces by characteristics and style – not by origin. In broad terms, there are seven main groups:

1 Old style. *This group of designs is derived from classical Rome, via the printers of Venice and Holland. It is very readable and looks good en masse. Examples: Garamond, Caslon.*
2 Modern. *Designed about 200 years ago to have greater mechanical perfection than old style faces. They have greater contrast between thick and thin strokes, finer serifs. Examples: Times Roman, Bodoni.*
3 Square serif. *A contemporary design, with square or blocked serifs, especially suitable for headlines or display. Example: Cheltenham.*
4 Sans serif. *A very simple modern typeface with no serifs and little contrast between thick and thin strokes. Examples: Gill, Helvetica.*
5 Script. *Imitates handwriting as on invitations. Examples: Palace, Shelley Allegro.*
6 Old English/Black Letter. *Imitates the Gothic handwriting of scribes writing out mediaeval scripts. Example: Old English.*
7 Decorative. *Novelty typefaces used mainly for display headlines or playbills. Examples: Comstock, Decorative.*

ABCDEFGHIJKLMNOPQRSTUVWX
abcdefghijklmnopqrstuvwxyzabcdefghijkl
OLD STYLE   GARAMOND

ABCDEFGHIJKLMNOPQRSTUVWX
abcdefghijklmnopqrstuvwxyzabcdefghijk
MODERN   TIMES ROMAN

ABCDEFGHIJKLMNOPQRSTUVWXYZAB
abcdefghijklmnopqrstuvwxyzabcdefghij
SQUARE SERIF   CHELTENHAM

ABCDEFGHIJKLMNOPQRSTUVWXYZ
abcdefghijklmnopqrstuvwxyzabcdefghijkl
SANS SERIF   HELVETICA

ABCDEFGHIJKLMNOPQ
abcdefghijklmnopqrstuvwxyzabcdefghijklmnopqrstuvwxyza
SCRIPT   SHELLEY ALLEGRO

𝔄𝔅ℭ𝔇𝔈𝔉𝔊ℌ𝕴𝔍𝔎𝔏𝔐𝔑𝔒𝔓𝔔ℜ𝔖𝔗𝔘
abcdefghijklmnopqrstuvwxyzabcdefg
BLACK FACE   OLD ENGLISH

ABCDEFGHIJKLMNOPQR
abcdefghijklmnopqrstuvw
DECORATIVE   COMSTOCK

U

Up-market. The other side of the coin to DOWN-MARKET – Harrods for shopping, Saabs for driving, the Cotswolds for living in, etc., all with one thing in common – that prices and profit margins are higher, which makes the thought of going up-market very attractive to many retailers and manufacturers. Quality ought to be higher too, but this doesn't always follow.

A brand does not necessarily have to be bought or used by people of high social status to become up-market. The up-market magic works much more powerfully by association. There are a number of mass-market brands which owe their success to being perceived as being used by people of high social status. Ponds (see TESTIMONIAL) was an early example of this. After Eight mints are a more recent one (see CASTING).

UPC. Universal Product Coding or, more usually, bar coding. The series of vertical lines on a pack which computers can read. For implications for the future, see EPOS.

USP. Unique Selling Proposition. Rosser Reeves' unique advertising model for the 1950s and the basis of the Ted Bates agency's success.★

Reeves' proposition is: 'The consumer tends to remember just one thing from an advertisement – one strong claim or one strong concept.' This has to be something the competition cannot offer and must be so strong that 'it can move the mass millions.' A famous example was Colgate Toothpaste: 'It cleans your breath while it cleans your teeth.'

The proposition is always verbal, rational, function-related – in effect a CONVERSION MODEL.

Since the sign of success in advertising was held to be people's ability to remember the proposition, it was easy to measure its effectiveness by RECALL TESTS.

Many agencies both sides of the Atlantic still like to clarify their thoughts with a USP (see PROPOSITION).

V

VALS. Values, Attitudes and Lifestyles. A psychographic cluster analysis devised by the Stanford Research Institute which adapts Maslow's Hierarchy of Needs model. People are typed according to where they are on the road to psychological maturity by the answers they give to attitude and social values questions, mostly by 5-point agree/disagree scales.

Young & Rubicam have combined this with product usage data to allow for segmentation analysis by attitudinal group. But as far as everyday household brands go, people seem to refuse to be neatly segmented (see MARKET SEGMENTATION). However, VALS may be more revealing on the more expensive and/or self-expressive purchases (e.g. cars, holidays, teenage essentials) as well as on broader questions such as politics or education.

See ATTITUDES/ATTITUDE RESEARCH, LIFESTYLE, PSYCHOGRAPHICS.

VCR. Videocassette-recorder. By the end of 1987, over 42 per cent of UK households had a VCR. BARB meters at present can detect when recording takes place and of what programme, and when something is being played back, but not what. This has a small effect on viewing figures for TV commercials. Are they watched twice (or more) – during recording and during every playback? Or not at all – if the recording is made for time-shift viewing and the commercial breaks zipped through on fast forward? At present there is no way of telling from the figures available. In a typical week (during the first quarter of 1987) an average of 4 hours 45 minutes of recording took place in a VCR home, and the average playback was 5 hours 15 minutes. This included rather more viewing of pre-recorded tapes, since we fail to view 20 per cent of what we record.* An experiment is under way for each programme and ad to be coded with a 'fingerprint' so BARB can meter each viewing whether live or taped.

Videotex. Another term for interactive VIDEOTEXT. Many videotex systems exist, mostly in private or restricted commercial use (e.g. Reuter's various financial data services). British Telecom's Prestel is the only national public videotex service in the UK. Signals are carried along telephone lines. Prestel, launched in 1979, still only reaches 40,000 households out of a total telephone usership of 74,000. Experiments in videotex services, like home shopping and tele-banking, have so far achieved little success. France's heavily-subsidized public videotex system, Minitel, which incorporates an electronic telephone directory, has been far more successful in reaching a mass market.

Videotext. Umbrella term for all methods of calling up computer pages for display on the TV set. A basic division exists between the broadcast version (TELETEXT) in which the viewer selects pages he wants out of a continuous broadcast cycle, and the interactive version (VIDEOTEX) in which he signals directly via cable or telephone wire. The structure of some cable and all telephone networks permits two-way, interactive use.

Viewing intensity. NRS classifies respondents by the hours they spend viewing any ITV channels which carry advertising:

Viewing intensity.

	Hours per week
Heavy viewing	20 hours +
Medium heavy	12–19.999 hours
Medium viewing	7–11.999 hours
Light medium	3–6.999 hours
Light viewing	1.5–2.9999 hours
Very light	0.001–1.4999 hours
'Never'	those who have no TV set, say they never watch ITV, TV–AM or Channel 4.

On average, we are 'heavy viewers', in the sense that the average viewing per week is over 20 hours. Even during the four weeks of the General Election in May 1987, when average viewing dropped 4 per cent, BARB showed it was still 22 hours 47 minutes per head.

Visual. How anything will/might/could look, e.g. a LAYOUT, a STORYBOARD, a photograph.

Visualizer. Stone-age word for ART DIRECTOR. Dates from the time when copy was written in one part of the agency and taken by a messenger to the art department for someone to 'visualize' and turn into a rough layout or poster. In those days the visualizer had to be able to draw, but only a few, like George Butler at JWT, rose above their station in the UK before the 1960s. Today the art director is in the ascendant, but never called visualizer.

Voice over. Indication, in film/TV script, of words to be spoken when the person speaking them (storyteller, salesman, housewife, voice of authority, etc.) is not seen to do so. MVO is male voice over, FVO is female voice over.

Voucher copy. Newspaper or magazine sent to the ad agency (or whoever is paying for the space) by the publisher to show where the advertisement actually appeared. Voucher copies are the record of the advertising kept in the GUARD BOOKS.

VTR. Video Tape Recording/Recorder. Action and sound for TV commercials are now often recorded on to magnetic tape – a cheaper alternative to film.

(Reprinted by kind permission of ADMAP)

Elizabeth Taylor, now appearing in
M.G.M.'s "The Light Fantastic,"
adores the way pure white Lux Toilet
Soap beautifies her skin.

"You can rely on this beauty soap
for a more lovely complexion"
says ELIZABETH TAYLOR

"My beauty method is really very
simple," says Elizabeth Taylor. "First,
I work up a wonderful white Lux
Toilet Soap lather."

". . . then I massage it into my face
using upward, circular movements.
Fatigue just floats away. I follow with
a warm rinse and cold splash."

"Finally, I pat dry. I know I can rely
on this method to keep my skin looking soft and alluring. Do try it. You'll
be as thrilled with the results as I am."

LUX TOILET SOAP is the beauty
choice of 9 out of 10 film
stars. They know that, because
its rich lather is as gentle and
effective as a beauty cream, Lux
Toilet Soap is able to give their
skin that important, deep-down
cleansing - without removing any
of the natural oils so essential to
beauty.

They find that this simple beauty
method described by Elizabeth
Taylor can be counted on to keep
their complexions always smooth
and perfect.

Lux Toilet Soap is composed
of the same blend of ingredients
as the finest French beauty soaps.
Try this method yourself. You'll
be thrilled to see how your skin
wakes up to an astonishing new
beauty.

9 out of 10 film stars use

LUX TOILET SOAP

A LEVER PRODUCT

LAURA LA PLANTE, *Universal*, says — "I've used many famous soaps, but I find Lux Toilet Soap gives my skin a marvellous smoothness"

CLARA BOW, *Paramount*—"Lux Toilet Soap is a great help in keeping the skin in perfect condition"

9 OUT OF 10
SCREEN STARS USE
LUX TOILET SOAP

for their exquisite, smooth skins

"SMOOTH SKIN ESSENTIAL," SAY LEADING DIRECTORS

"Smooth, exquisite skin is essential for popularity," leading motion picture directors declare. "It has a universal appeal," they say. "No film star can attain success on the screen without it."

Every star in Hollywood and England knows that only smooth, perfect skin can successfully meet the all-revealing glare of the Klieg lights in the close-up.

Nine out of ten screen stars use Lux Toilet Soap! There are in Hollywood and England 714 important film actresses — including all stars — 98% care for their skin with this lovely, fragrant white soap.

And the great film studios, following their stars' example, have made Lux Toilet Soap the official soap in all their studio dressing-rooms. Beauty is important in filmland!

You, too, will be delighted with the delicate bloom of your skin when Lux Toilet Soap cares for it. Order some today. All grocers and stores have it. Lever Brothers Limited, Port Sunlight.

BEBE DANIELS, lovely *Paramount* star —"The girl with smooth skin need not fear the searching lens of the close-up. Lux Toilet Soap is a great help in keeping the skin smooth and lovely"

*All the big film studios
have made Lux Toilet Soap
the official soap in their
dressing-rooms*   4ᴰ

Lux Toilet Soap has been a world brand since the 1920s. Very early on the advertising was based on the testimony of Hollywood film stars who had already become the symbols for beauty throughout the world wherever a cinema had opened. The ad above featuring Laura La Plante, Clara Bow and Bebe Daniels is pre-1940. Elizabeth Taylor opposite appeared in the early 1950s. The campaign was adapted to markets in different parts of the world by using the stars who were most popular there. With acknowledgements and thanks to Lever Brothers Limited.

W

Wear out. A rather imprecise way of describing when an advertisement or commercial ceases to generate effective response from its TARGET GROUP. The term is normally applied to the number of times each individual ad or commercial can stand being exposed within the schedule. There is no objective way of measuring this. It is a matter of judgement and judging by the way some commercials are screened *ad nauseam*, even judgement is not being exercised. See also ADSTOCK, CARRYOVER.

Web-offset. Literally, lithographic printing on to a roll (or web) of paper at high speed. Offset because the image is not directly printed but offset via a system of cylinders and rubber 'blankets' (the numbers of which vary depending on the machine and how many colours it can print on the same run) on to the paper.

Web-offset presses are widely used for high-quality colour work (travel brochures, catalogues), colour printing on cheap paper (newspapers) and speed.

Weekly reach. The number of potential listeners who listen to their commercial radio station at any time during an average week. This is expressed as a percentage or in thousands and related to the total of a particular universe.

Weighting. Statistical term for attaching greater or lesser importance to a particular factor. Widely used in media and market research, e.g. to match up a TARGET GROUP to NRS figures, or a SAMPLE with its demographic characteristics.

White goods. CONSUMER DURABLES which used to be available only in white – or most daringly cream – and so called on the assumption that everything in the kitchen would be white. But, even though all-white kitchens become the rage again from time to time, 'white goods' are now also available in almost any colour. The term covers most gas and electric appliances: washing machines, dryers, vacuum cleaners, cookers, refrigerators, freezers, microwave ovens, dishwashers.

See BROWN GOODS.

World brands. Brands with world-wide sales and acceptance. So-called world brands include: Coca Cola, Pepsi, Kodak, Kelloggs, Rolex, Mercedes, Levis, Sony, IBM – all marketed by multinational companies. One or two come near to GLOBAL ADVERTISING (same brand, same advertising everywhere) strategies. Most are more flexible, and even when the BRAND STRATEGY and the BRAND PERSONALITY are set at head office, the advertising is developed and adapted to local needs and circumstances, usually by local people. The three brands illustrated here are examples of world brands which adapt their advertising in this way.

Z

Zapping. Using the remote control to flick from one TV channel to another during the commercial break.

Zoom. Technically a lens for a camera with a variable focal length. 'Zoom in' is a non-technical way to describe the effect of moving very quickly from a general shot into the close-up of a detail.

Two recent Marlboro ads from their campaign which features the archetypal Wild West – thanks to Hollywood the cowboy, like the film star, is a potent metaphor throughout the world. The success of Marlboro as a world brand owes much to this campaign, invented over thirty years ago by Leo Burnett. It transformed the brand personality from a filter tip cigarette designed for women (with a pink tip to conceal the lipstick smears) to the strong masculine brand it is today. The campaign runs with slightly different emphasis in different parts of the world depending on culture and legislation (see CIGARETTES for what is allowed in the UK). Some markets respond more to the country, others to the cowboy. Although from time to time ethnic cowboys have been featured, the rugged all-American features of this cowboy have been found to have universal appeal. Strategy and creative approach are initiated in the US, while the advertisements are adapted in each country to meet local regulations and preferences.

References

Introduction
★ J. P. Wood, 'The story of advertising', quoted in T. R. Nevitt, *Advertising in Britain* (Heinemann, 1982).
† James Webb Young, *How to Become an Advertising Man* (Advertising Publications Inc., 1963).
Account planner
★ Roy Langmaid, 'A psycho–dynamic perspective on the rise of account planning', *ADMAP*, April 1985.
Advertisement
★ Jeremy Bullmore, 'Advertising: what is it', from the *Advertising Association Handbook* (Holt, Rinehart and Winston, 1983).
Advertising agency
★ Charles Channon, 'Agency thinking and agencies as brands', *ADMAP*, March 1981.
Advertising Effectiveness Awards
★ *Advertising Works 1:* ed. Simon Broadbent (Holt, Rinehart and Winston, 1981); *Advertising Works 2:* ed. Simon Broadbent (Holt, Rinehart and Winston, 1983); *Advertising Works 3:* ed. Charles Channon (Holt, Rinehart and Winston, 1985); *Advertising Works 4:* ed. Charles Channon (Holt, Rinehart and Winston, 1987).
Advertising idea
★ David Ogilvy, *Ogilvy on Advertising* (Pan Books, 1983).
† James Webb Young, *A Technique for Producing Ideas* (Advertising Publications Inc., 1946).
‡ David Bernstein, *Creative Advertising: for this you went to Oxford?* (Longman, 1974).
★★ Barry Day ed. *100 Great Advertisements* (Times Newspapers, Mirror Group, *Campaign,* 1978).
Attitudes/Attitude research
★ M. Brewster Smith, *Attitude Change,* reprinted in *Attitudes,* eds Neil Warren and Marie Jahoda (Penguin Books, 1966).
Brand image
★ David Ogilvy (1974) op. cit.

212

Brand personality
★ Stephen King, *What is a Brand?* (J. Walter Thompson Co. Ltd, 1970).

Cognitive dissonance
★ L. Festinger, *A Theory of Cognitive Dissonance* (Stanford University Press, 1957).

Consumer movement
★ Alan Wolfe, *Public Attitudes to Advertising* (AA Handbook) (Holt, Rinehart and Winston, 1983).

Consumers
★ Wendy Gordon and Colleen Ryan, 'How do consumers feel advertising works?', MRS Conference, 1983.

Copywriter
★ David Ogilvy, op. cit.

Corporate advertising
★ David Bernstein, *Company Image and Reality* (Holt, Rinehart and Winston, 1984).

† W. Olins, *The Corporate Personality* (The Design Council, 1978).

‡ Theodore Levitt, 'Communications and industrial selling', *Journal of Marketing,* April 1967.

★★ Alan Wolfe, 'How to adapt research techniques to design and assess corporate image advertising' (ESOMAR, 1978); also in *Corporate Advertising* (IPA, 1983).

†† Stephen King, 'Public response: the key to corporate advertising', *Advertising*, Winter 1978–9; also in *Corporate Advertising* (IPA, 1983).

DAGMAR
★ Russell Colley, *Defining Advertising Goals for Measured Advertising Results* (Association of National Advertisers, 1961).

Direct response
★ Claude Hopkins, *Scientific Advertising* (originally published 1923; reissued Moore, 1952; MacGibbon & Kee, 1968).

Evaluation
★ Stephen King, 'Practical progress from a theory of advertisements', *ADMAP,* Vol.11, No.10, October 1975, pp.338–43.

† Jeremy Elliott, 'Campaign evaluation' in *How to Plan Advertising*, D. Cowley ed. (Cassell, 1987). Condensed from Roger Clayton, Estelle Williams and Rick Bendel, 'Building a business through advertising: Zanussi', *Advertising Works 3*, IPA, 1985.

Extended group
- ★ Peter Sampson, 'Qualitative and motivation research' from Robert M. Worcester and John Downham eds *Consumer Market Research Handbook* (North-Holland for ESOMAR, 1986).

Geodemographics
- ★ R.J. Webber, 'The national classification of residential neighbourhoods – an introduction to the classification of wards and parishes', *PRAG Technical Papers*, No TP 23 (Centre for Environmental Studies, 1977).

Global advertising
- ★ Theodore Levitt, 'The globalization of markets', *Harvard Business Review,* May/June 1983.
- † Sir John Harvey Jones, from an address to the American Chamber of Commerce (UK). 21 January 1988.

Headline
- ★ Claude Hopkins, op. cit.

Housewife
- ★ 'Shopping by Male' (Mirror Group Newspapers (1986) Ltd, 1987).

Hypethetico–deductive methodology
- ★ Jeremy Bullmore, 'What is Creativity?, *Adweek* 19 January 1973. 'Archimedes and the efficacy of prayer' (address to the Account Planning Group, November 1985).

Innovation
- ★ Stephen King, *Developing New Brands* (Pitman, 1973).

International advertising
- ★ Harold F. Clark Jr, 'Consumer and corporate values: yet another view on global marketing', *International Journal of Advertising,* 1987.
- † Roderick White, *Advertising – what it is and how to do it* (McGraw-Hill, 1980).

Lateral thinking
- ★ Edward de Bono, *The Use of Lateral Thinking* (Jonathan Cape 1967).

Lifestyles
- ★ Donald Monk, 'Burnett Life Style Research', *European Research,* (1973).
- † T. Lunn, S. Baldwin and J. Dickens, 'Monitoring consumer life styles', *ADMAP*, November 1972.

‡ K. Baker and R. Fletcher, 'Outlook – a generalised lifestyle system', *ADMAP*, March 1987.

Market segmentation

★ John Philip Jones, *What's in a Name?* (D.C. Heath & Co., 1986).

Marketing myopia

★ Theodore Levitt, 'Marketing myopia', *Harvard Business Review*, July/August 1960.

Metaphor

★ David Bernstein (1974) op. cit.

NRS

★ Simon Broadbent and Brian Jacobs, *Spending Advertising Money* (Hutchinson, 1984).

Packaging

★ David Bernstein (1974) op. cit.

Promotion

★ Stephen King (1974) op. cit.

Psychographics

★ William D. Wells and Douglas J. Tigert, 'Activities, interests and opinions', *Journal of Advertising Research*, 1971.

† Ken Baker and Robert Fletcher, 'Outlook – a generalized lifestyle system', *ADMAP*, March 1987.

Public relations

★ David Bernstein (1984) op. cit.

Questionnaire

★ S.L. Payne, *The Art of Asking Questions* (Princeton University Press, 1951).

Readership

★ Herbert E. Krugman, 'Memory without recall, exposure without perception', *Journal of Advertising Research*, August 1977.

Reinforcement

★ Alan Hedges, *Testing to Destruction* (IPA, 1974).

Repertoire

★ A.S.C. Ehrenberg, *Repeat-buying, Theory and Applications* (North-Holland, 1972).

Role for advertising

★ Dr Timothy Joyce, 'What do we know about how advertising works?', ESOMAR seminar, Noordwijk, May 1987.

† Stephen King (1975) op. cit.

‡ Alan Hedges, op. cit.

** Judie Lannon and Peter Cooper, 'Humanistic advertising', *International Journal of Advertising,* 1983.

Sensitivity panel

* Linda Fuller, 'Use of panels for qualitative research', *Journal of Market Research Society,* vol. 26/3, 1984.

† W. Schlackman, 'A discussion of the use of sensitivity panels in market research', *Journal of Market Research Society,* vol, 26/3, 1984.

Stimulus and response theory

* Arthur Koestler, *The Act of Creation,* (Hutchinson, 1964).

Target groups

* Simon Broadbent ed. (1981) op. cit.

† Stephen Benson of Davidson Pearce for Van den Berghs, winner of First Prize and Grand Prix, First Advertising Effectiveness Awards, 1981.

USP

* Rosser Reeves, *Reality in Advertising* (Knopf, 1961).

VCR

* Pamela Reiss, 'TV audiences: VCRs as the fifth dimension', *ADMAP,* November 1987.